MW01702236

DEANN (WOLKOW) KRUEMPEL

Leaving a Trail

First published by DeAnn Kruempel 2024

Copyright © 2024 by DeAnn (Wolkow) Kruempel

All rights reserved. No part of this publication may be reproduced, stored or transmitted in any form or by any means, electronic, mechanical, photocopying, recording, scanning, or otherwise without written permission from the publisher. It is illegal to copy this book, post it to a website, or distribute it by any other means without permission.

First edition

ISBN: 978-1-952891-14-4

This book was professionally typeset on Reedsy.
Find out more at reedsy.com

Leaving a Trail is dedicated to all who struggle with memory loss. I pray that in some small way, these stories will brighten the days and lighten the burdens of you and your loved ones. May these memories inspire you to share yours and leave your own trail.

"Love never fails..."
1 Corinthians 13:8

Contents

Foreword

Welcome to Leaving a Trail, named for one of my favorite quotes: "Do not follow where the path may lead. Go instead where there is no path and leave a trail." Ralph Waldo Emerson and Muriel Strode are both credited for this bit of inspirational wisdom.

This book includes memories of growing up on the farm, though some may take a slightly different twist. I hope you enjoy the stories as much as those in my previous books, *Once Upon a Midwest Sunset*, *Putting on the Big Boots* and *Back to Forward.*

May the stories bring back your own precious memories!

Acknowledgments

Thank you to my siblings, Deloris, Darlene, Dorothy and Delmer. Your willingness to share your memories makes it fun to write about them. A text or phone call away, I hope you realize how much I treasure your constant support and encouragement.

Thank you, Dorothy, for being my editor and sounding board every week. Comma usage still baffles me!

To our niece Susan, your photos bring back so many precious memories. Thank you for your willingness to help! Some pictures appear in this book. They inspire more stories!

Thank you to the staff at the Harrison County Museum and Welcome Center, Missouri Valley Iowa, for your support and your help with photographs at your wonderful museum.

To all the newspapers who print my columns, thank you for getting our stories into the homes of thousands of readers. The memories live on!

I

Part One

Chapter 1

The Disappearing Link

Our dad took tons of pictures. Birthdays, new babies, new cars. "I want to get a picture," he would tell his brothers when they visited with their families. "Everyone, line up here by the car." Thus, we can smile at a whole line of cousin pictures the cousins don't even have!

Dad's first camera was a black box. No flash, but outside pictures worked just fine. There was a film inside the camera and the photographer needed to remember to wind forward for the next picture. The film, then black and white, had to be developed. Drug stores often offered film processing, and you paid per print. If the print was a dark blob or a sheet of white, you still paid; people were careful not to waste pictures.

New photo technology evolved and soon visitors and family members appeared in colored prints. Flash cubes allowed indoor images, and Christmas tree portraits and kitchen table projects were added to albums.

Along came the Polaroid camera! Dad would pull the white plastic coated square out of the camera with a flourish, wait a few seconds and then peel back the filmy sheet. We all watched in amazement as the photo developed before our eyes.

Did our father know that someday those photographs he took would be precious to his children? Did he realize that many would evoke memories of special times and special people as we scan through them?

Today people take megatons of pictures. Finish lines, playgrounds, zoos, restaurants, hunting grounds, dining room tables. Cell phones and digital cameras provide a quick, easy way to capture the moment. They can send it to other cell phones so that people all over the world can see the picture on the tiny screen in their hand. Amazing!

But advances in technology come with a price. We take a giant leap forward in one area, but scoot backward a major step in another. Millions, probably billions of photos are stored in phones. It is fun to access a recent take and proudly present it to the person nearby. It is easy to post on social media for the world to see. But sometimes phones get lost or the photos get erased, much to the dismay of the owner. Or the sheer quantity of accessible pictures prohibits Ooh! and Ah! Moments.

Few people print out photos anymore. How do I know? Try buying a photo album. Big box stores don't carry them. Even albums one can order from the giant catalogs in the sky are limited.

In twenty years will children be able to page through an album or flip through prints? Will they be able to hold that tangible piece of history in their hands and remember?

This is our chance to leave a trail. Specialty stores still print photos. We can select the most precious and have them converted to more permanent pieces. We can buy albums for grandchildren and fill them with new prints every year. Their smiles as they turn the pages make it worth every penny, every second invested.

Printed photos are a link to the past. To people and events. To memories and stories and smiles. To history. Let's not let the link disappear.

Chapter 2

Going "Spoonless"

"I picked up a watermelon in Huron. Thought it would taste good in this heat." Mom nodded a smile of thanks to her husband, already looking forward to the cool, sweet treat.

"The kids will love it!" She didn't mention her newly finished kitchen floor that shined like a mirror, but Dad didn't miss much.

That night after supper, he sent Donald down to the tank where the melon chilled in the cold artesian water. Mom's always-sharp butcher knife made quick work of slicing. "If it splits ahead of the knife, it's a good one." She stacked the bright red and dark green half circles in a cake pan and the family headed out to the five-by-eight wooden platform next to the front door, a wide step we called "the stoop."

The delightful watermelon scent greeted me as I hunted for the slice that looked like it had the least seeds. I thought I had hit the jackpot, but discovered there were extra on the opposite side. Soon we all sat on the step, savoring the juicy sweetness. My shorts and shirt soaked up the pink liquid, as the juice dripped from my chin. "Mom, we should raise watermelon in the garden!" I pictured great striped-green orbs snuggled into lush vines; there would be so many we could eat watermelon every night for weeks!

"This one came from a place in Nebraska," Dad told us between bites. "They have sandy soil, just right for raising watermelons. We'd have to water them a lot here."

I felt a small seed slide down my throat and was thinking someone should invent a watermelon without seeds. Just then Donald poked Delmer with his elbow. "Bet I can spit the seeds farther than you can!"Not one to refuse a challenge, Delmer beamed his silver-laced grin and aimed one that arched up and landed in the grass five feet away. Soon black spotted seeds flew wildly into the fence line. Family laughter blended with farm sounds on that warm South Dakota night.

Delmer and I gazed at the two slices remaining in the pan. "Don't eat too much or you will wet the bed." I huffed a sigh of disappointment at Mom's gentle reminder.

"Sure hope no one swallowed any seeds," Dad said as he tossed empty rinds into the chicken treat bucket. "You know they can grow in your stomach."

My eyes shot to my father's, hoping to see that mischievous twinkle, but he seemed pretty serious. I looked to Mom, thinking she might be grinning and shaking her head at her husband's teasing, but she had headed into the house.

No watermelons grew in my tummy that summer, but some shot up in the front yard the next spring. The precious memories still frolic in my head.

Today most store-bought watermelons are seedless, (Be careful what you wish for!) so we would need to improvise on the seed-spitting. But we can still eat melons outside without spoons. We can think of ordinary events and make them extraordinary, like planting watermelons with a grandchild or shelling an ear of popcorn and popping it in a kettle. (How many youngsters think popcorn has to come in a microwave bag?)

These uncomplicated efforts may seem trivial at the time, but who knows? We may be leaving a cherished trail of memories!

Chapter 3

Crowning Glory—Highlights of a Lifetime

Our grandma braided her hair and wound it in a tight circle at the crown of her head. Bobby pins must have secured that braid, though I never saw them. As a child I imagined this as her permanent hairstyle.

In Mom's wedding portrait her hair is parted on one side and waved deeply on the other. Likely, her sisters helped style her hair for the special day. At the time there was no electricity, but there were curling irons and crimpers! The metal curling part heated on the stove. Wooden handles allowed the stylist to wrap the hair into wonderful waves. One iron heated while the other curled. Women marveled at the dazzling technology available for training tresses.

A few years and quite a few hairstyles later, Mom had four daughters. We dreamed of the latest "do" and procured the essential provisions. Brush rollers in every size filled sparkly tubs on our dressers along with pink plastic pokey things. Soon we added pastel-colored cylinders and giant bobby pins. Pomade and curling gel set curls to endure cheering sessions.

Teasing combs teased. (Mom called it ratting; Dad made subtle hints of rats' nests!) Gallons of Aqua Net permitted tornado tress testing. Or if we wanted serious curls, we bought a home permanent wave and the skinny rods to go with it.

Armed with the necessities, we worked on those waves. Since we had no shower, the girls washed our hair in the small porcelain sink in the kitchen. That drain was easier for Dad to clean than the tub. Having shampooed and conditioned and combed, we painstakingly rolled sections of wet hair onto the rollers and poked in pins or metal clasps. Giant sheer scarves tied on top kept the rollers in place while we worked or studied. If neighbor boys came over to see Delmer, we hid. The alien look was reserved for family. And get this, quite often it was required that we sleep on those things! It didn't matter; lovely locks required pain and suffering.

Hair fashions through the ages have been influenced by the celebrities of the time: Audrey Hepburn, Dorothy Hamill, Cher, Farrah Fawcett. Consider the coifs, cuts and colors that have highlighted our generation. Big hair. Little hair. There was a time when almost every girl dreamed of a "flip." Bouffants, beehives, bobs and bowls brushed with pageboys, shags and spikes. Later, we decided curls required straightening.

The recent pandemic mandated isolation. Beauty shops closed and there bounced up stories to curl your hair! People cut their own or let it grow. After all, no one would see them anyway! But the kids were home all the time and always getting in the folks' hair. Some said it was enough to make them tear their hair out. Even the children argued about every little thing, like splitting hairs.

Today, still more styles have become rooted in history. Symmetry is no longer required. Every color of the rainbow is available and can be changed with the sunset. Gray hair is justly considered "wisdom highlights."

A very thoughtful means of leaving a trail is to donate long hair to organizations that make wigs for cancer patients. Ask your hairdresser for details. Do you leave a trail for the vacuum and dustpan? Don't tear out your hair over it. Toss it in the compost pile!

Life's highlights can make every day a good hair day.

Chapter 4

No Idle Threats

"Get in the car right now, or I'm leaving without you!" The man yelled at two youngsters who continued to tear through the playground. I refrained from telling him that idle threats were ineffective child rearing techniques. Kids figure out in a hurry that those adults don't really mean what they are saying; it's not rocket science. Although, I do remember a family of eight driving off after church in Toeterville, Iowa and leaving one of their brood behind. The dad showed up an hour later to collect the boy. It only happened once.

Growing up on the farm, our parents often attached an incentive to their directives, but they knew better than to tell us lies. Yes sirree, Bob! Every thing our parents told us was totally true!

"Eat spinach, it will make you strong!" Well, it certainly worked for Popeye!

"Carrots help you see in the dark...Take this spoon of castor oil so you don't get sick...An apple a day keeps the doctor away... Chicken soup helps fight a cold."

Occasionally, the toaster would get a bit over-zealous and the slice would pop up totally blackened. Not wanting to waste anything, Dad informed us that "eating burnt toast put hair on your chest." Don and Delmer may have buttered and bit in with relish. I quickly discovered our dog Rex wanted a hairy chest.

Some of the folks' behavior-adjusting tactics included the obvious results of neglect. "Brush your teeth, or this is what happens!" Dad popped out his dentures to prove the point.

Mom often instructed me to "wash behind your ears, or the dirt will grow in." I must have failed, as I remember her scrubbing away as if cottonwoods were sprouting in the accumulation. "When you swallow gum, it stays in your stomach forever." I never found proof that it didn't, so it had to be true!

"Coffee stunts your growth." Maxing out at 5' 1", I must have drunk too much of that!

"If you sit too close to the TV, you will damage your eyes." I envisioned dark glasses and walking with a mobility cane, cautiously tapping in front of me. I did not sit close to the TV. (Upon researching this admonition, I learned that there was a period of time when televisions emitted harmful radiation. For whatever reason, it was good we kept a distance.)

"If you keep crossing your eyes, they will stay that way." Hey, it works with memory foam! "Don't tell a lie or your nose will grow." That was a no-brainer; look at Pinocchio!

From somewhere in my memory banks comes the phrase, "Put on clean underwear in case you're in an accident." Always a good rule to follow!

"Good night. Sleep tight. Don't let the bedbugs bite." As a child, I sighed in weary contentment at the silly rhyme and drifted off. Not until I was nearly 60 years old did I learn that bedbugs really exist and that they are horrible creatures!

Of course, youngsters notice parental strategies and try similar techniques on their younger siblings. "You had better behave or the bogeyman will get you!" Delmer claims his older sisters came up with this to scare him into compliance. I think he invented it to terrorize his little sister. It didn't work.

Just what is a bogeyman, anyway?

Chapter 5

Smells Like Work!

I stepped off the school bus to a farmyard bustling with activity. A tractor pulled a trailer behind the barn. A scraping sound blended with the engine noises. A hint of fall hovered in the cool South Dakota air, blended with something else—the distinct smell of silage.

A herd of stock cows roamed our pastures during warmer months, but wintered in the yards close to the barn. Silage topped the list on their winter menu, so Dad, Donald and Delmer made sure plenty of the feed was stored up.

In October, a neighbor brought his chopper and wagons, and the men worked to "put up silage." In early years the chopper was a single row, but still the pile grew. Like many things on the farm back then, silage meant work. The fermented feed had to be hauled to the cattle. During times when the loader was attached to a tractor, the men scooped and hauled to the feed bunks. But when the loader was not available, the guys used the silage fork to fill a galvanized, rope-handled bushel-basket with the feed.

We were taught to put away tools and equipment, but the 14-tine fork and the big old basket waited right next to the silage pile. Why haul it to the barn when you were going to need it again in a few hours? When there were two men doing chores, one scooped the silage into the basket and carried it to the board fence. The other waited on the other side. He pulled the heavy container down from the fence top and emptied it into bunks for the weaned calves. Sometimes, one guy worked alone. He had to balance the huge basket on the fence while climbing over.

Delmer also recalls scooping the sweet-sour-smelling silage onto the hay rack and pulling it behind the 520 John Deere tractor out to the cattle yards. There he scooped it one more time, into the bunk or tractor tire feeders. The cattle sniffed and waited for dinner with eager anticipation.

The problem with a silage pile was the waste. Where air touched the chopped-up corn, the fermentation process went awry and the outer crust spoiled. The spoiled layer did not have the sweet-sour pickled smell. It smelled like something else that went into the manure spreader, which is where the guys dumped it.

To save on spoilage, the men built a bunker silo. Even the building process was labor-intensive. Dad, Don and Delmer mixed cement in small batches, hauled it in the wheelbarrow and dumped and leveled it between the two pre-made cement walls. Hundreds of cement bags, messy batches and wheelbarrow loads eventually formed a floor on which to store the following years' batches of silage.

Cows and calves thrived on the savory fermented feed. Their stomachs, all four sections, benefitted from "gut health," a result of all the probiotics and fiber in the pickled product. Today there are probably fewer farmers who lug bushel baskets to their calf feeders. Silage wagons and tractor loaders carry much of the load. But that distinct scent of fermenting silage still permeates crisp fall mornings. The cows and calves still lift their noses and wait in eager anticipation, and the farmer still thinks it smells like work!

Chapter 6

The Best Things in Life

When I was pretty close to being a teenager, I decided I wanted a small transistor radio. I don't recall if my friends had them, but for some reason I NEEDED to own that small box of sound I could take anywhere.

The invention of the transistor in the early 1950s paved the way for mass-produced pocket radios. A transistor is a pencil-eraser-sized device that generates and amplifies electric signals. Transistors eliminated the need for bulky vacuum tubes and the restriction of having to be close to an electrical outlet. In 1959 six million transistor radios were imported from Japan; I was not the first kid to think I needed the invention.

As the youngest and most spoiled in the family, I felt no qualms about letting Mom and Dad know when I wanted something. Likely, my hints were not too subtle, and low-and-behold, on my next birthday I was thoroughly thrilled to hold that coveted contraption in my grubby little paws.

Mine was a white plastic box encased in black vinyl. A flimsy vinyl ribbon handle curved over the top. Two notched circles peeked out from the plastic cover, one on each side. These were perfect for turning with index fingers. One adjusted volume. One tuned into radio stations. I learned from my older sisters that KOMA was the hip station for rock and roll music. With a 50,000-watt signal, the station attracted teens.

I unsnapped the plastic case, opened the box and popped in the nine-volt battery. Life was good! I sat on the front step and cranked up the sound. The dog and cats gathered around me. Paul Revere and the Raiders belted out "Louie Louie." No one was around to tell me to turn down the volume. Shep did turn his head to the side as if wondering why I would listen to anything with such poor sound quality.

Tucked into the egg bucket, the small radio played Herman's Hermits' "I'm Henry the VIII I am" for the chickens. All but three committed clucks evacuated the coop. Obviously, chickens did not appreciate good music.

After supper, the Beach Boys made "Good Vibrations" in front of my math textbook as I did homework at the kitchen table. That night I turned the volume down low so Mom and Dad would not hear, and set my precious radio on the pillow next to me. I sighed in contentment, serenaded with "Hey Mr. Tambourine Man." Dino, Desi and Billy would have been disappointed to know that I fell asleep during their top hit song.

The next morning, I woke up to see my wonderful birthday present still on the pillow. Frowning at its silence, I turned the volume button. No sound piped up. I frantically tried to tune in a different station. Nothing. I had depleted the battery in less than 24 hours!

The next day, I replaced the battery and again kept the radio next to me at every private moment. That night I fell asleep again and drained another battery. I had a sinking feeling that the folks were not going to be happy about buying nine-volts in bulk.

A week later I found an electric AM-FM radio sitting on the table next to my bed. Amazingly, it found KOMA and played the same tunes. I turned it down at night and listened to music as I drifted off to sleep. Realizing it was not so great after all, I tucked that small transistor into my bottom dresser drawer.

Our parents knew from the get-go what would happen when I got the transistor I wanted so badly. They could have told me I didn't need it; it was a waste of money. But they didn't. They understood that there are some lessons children need to learn on their own in life—lessons like the best things in life aren't things.

Chapter 7

When Pictures Came Through Our Ears

By the time I came along, the Golden Age of Radio had faded to silver or bronze; television took over as the primary broadcast media. But the radio in our South Dakota farm kitchen continued to inform and entertain for many years.

Every weekday, housewives throughout the Midwest were greeted with "Hello there, good friends." The voice of Wynn Speece, WNAX radio's reliable neighbor lady. She delivered recipes, hints and words of advice. Mom tuned in the radio early in the morning, but kept the volume on low until she heard the familiar voice. As the youngest, most spoiled in the family, I don't remember many times when I was hushed, but when Mom was copying a recipe for beef stroganoff from "The Neighbor Lady," she held her ear close to the brown plastic sound box and I was expected to be quiet.

Speece broadcast live shows, sometimes from her own dining room table, featuring letters from listeners, interviews with celebrities and tips for homemakers.

Iowa listened to a similar radio show from WHO radio in Des

Moines. The show was dubbed "Kitchen Klatter." The voice was Leanna Field Driftmier. Leanna sometimes counseled listeners on childrearing and, like Speece, offered household hints and recipes.

Our radio was dark brown plastic. It was about twelve inches long and seven inches high and wide, and was powered by electricity. The edges were rounded and the top curved slightly. Turning knobs on the side adjusted the volume and the station. A vertical red bar glided over numbers on the top front, indicating the call numbers of the station. The remaining front served as a speaker.

The device provided the latest news. Both of our parents often listened for the daily grain market report and recorded it in a seed corn book. Occasionally, the figures resulted in a load of oats or corn being hauled to the Erwin or De Smet elevator.

Mom found a station that broadcast a church service in Swedish. Dorothy recalls asking our mother if she could speak Swedish. Mom replied that she could not speak it very well any more, but she could still understand the words. Often, she hummed along with the hymns.

Delmer distinctly remembers the narrator and theme song as the Lone Ranger galloped into our kitchen on a late winter afternoon. Once we sat down to supper, Mom switched off the radio. Back then parents knew the importance of family time and communication.

Before electricity, frontier families gathered around bulky wooden boxes and "cathedral" radios, which were the source of national news as well as entertainment. Our dear 103-year-old Ethel remembers her mother listening to her favorite radio program, "One Man's Family."

Batteries in those old radios were expensive and money was

hard to come by. Listening time was limited to a few select hours every week. Likely, they enjoyed every minute!

Sometimes in a conversation with a much younger person, reminiscing the past, he or she will ask, "How did you manage back in the old days? How could you live without modern devices like big screen TVs?"

I simply smile and reply, "We made the best of what we had. We adapted to the technology of the time. I never felt like I was missing out on anything."

Hmmm. I wonder if those are the thoughts of every generation as they remember their growing up years?

Old, old radio

Chapter 8

Check Your Surroundings

My car talks to me! No, unfortunately, this relationship is nothing like that of Herbie, the Love Bug. To be honest, I didn't notice this message from my vehicle until I had driven her at least a year. When I put my "Little Honder" in reverse the backup camera screen flashes on my dash with the image of what lies behind. At the bottom of that screen in small white letters, it says, "Check your surroundings."

Fall is my favorite season. Every year I resolve to take more time to enjoy the colors of the leaves, the unfamiliar songs of the migrating birds as they flit through my yard, the beauty in the flowing grasses as they bend in the breeze. Every year I see it and smile—-for about a minute. The next day, it seems, the wind wreaks havoc and I look up to see bare branches and empty skies. Obviously, I blinked.

Remembering our parents and the way we lived as I was growing up, there is something that totally baffles me. In my opinion, they worked harder, accomplished far more and sat much less than me. But they still managed to enjoy the beauty around them. They still managed to find the time to cherish life.

There were those Sunday drives—the slow treks over less-traveled roads with no destination in mind. But, oh boy did those drives have a purpose. Every one of us in that car focused on the windows. What kind of ducks were those bobbing in the slough? A gangling pelican plunged into the water nearby. Seven young pheasants skittered behind mother hen as they crossed the gravel road in front of us. The folks noted every field and pasture. Dad graded the quality of beef as the cattle grazed in the distance. I don't think I ever turned down a chance for a Sunday drive.

Mom loved flowers; the splotches of color throughout the garden and yard proved it. Though her daily work routine rivaled her farmer husband and sons, she took the time to enjoy and share the beauty. A bouquet of cosmos, zinnias, glads or "rooster combs" graced our kitchen table from early spring through frost.

"Let's take a walk through the shelter belt." We might scout for asparagus or wild plums or watch a doe and fawn bound through the underbrush. Sometimes leaves crunched under our shoes. I remember Mom spotting a giant cottonwood leaf. She picked it up and placed the golden heart in my hands. "You can press this in the old encyclopedias. It will keep for a long time." That fall and many years following, crisp flat leaves of scarlet, yellow and orange fell from the heavy books as I ruffled through the pages.

"DeAnn, come outside, I want to show you something." Dad's eyes twinkled as he peeked into the kitchen. In the front yard, in the lowest crotch of the boxelder tree, a robin glared from her mud-cement nest. As a small child, I thrilled at the wonder of life as I watched from my father's shoulders.

Did the people of our parents' generation have some deeper understanding of nature and the urgency of sharing this with their children? Or had they learned lessons from life? Were there times when every ounce of energy, every waking second needed to be used for survival? Or were there years that were so full of worry and sadness that they missed the chances to enjoy life?

I can only imagine, for each person's trials are different. But I do know that somehow my siblings and I learned to cherish nature and life.

Cars didn't "talk" back then, but people didn't seem to need any reminders to check their surroundings. Possibly that generation read the wisdom of Ralph Waldo Emerson: "Never lose an opportunity of seeing anything beautiful, for beauty is God's handwriting."

Maybe. But I like to think they just knew it.

Chapter 9

Laughter is the Best Medicine. That's No Joke!

The little girl watched as he slipped his arms into his going-to-town jacket. The man lifted his hat from the hook behind the door. "Where are you going, Daddy?"

His hazel eyes twinkled as he looked down at his precious six-year-old child. "Crazy! Want to come along?" Dorothy's blond braids bounced as she hurried to get her own good coat.

Our parents both had a sense of humor. Dad, especially, felt the need to make us laugh. My siblings and I all recall some of the same silly quips; he must have repeated them through the years. A drive to town, the trek to the barn for chores, or sitting around the supper table were all prime times for stories:

"Young James went off to college. Well, college life did not go as well as he had expected. After weeks of neglecting his studies and frittering away Daddy's cash, James found himself a little down on his luck. Finally, he didn't know what else to do, so he penned a brief note to his father. 'No mon. No fun. Your son.' His wise, unsympathetic parent quickly shot back a blunt reply: 'Too bad. Sure sad. Your dad.'"

Then there was Little Johnny. Dad's stories of the precocious boy never failed to produce a smile. Do you remember this one? "Little Johnny's teacher assigned him to use four new vocabulary words in a sentence: defeat, deduct, defense and detail. Johnny barely batted an eye as he met the challenge. 'De feet of de duck went over de fence before de tail!"

Knock knock jokes? Ole and Lena stories? As a Swede, Mom mimicked the distinctive Norwegian brogue very well. But sometimes she got into the story and started laughing so hard that she couldn't finish. Gathered around the kitchen table, tears streamed down her sisters' faces and their bodies shook. The hilarity must have been contagious, as all of us laughed uncontrollably without even hearing the end of the story!

Every weekend Mom cut out cartoons from the paper, particularly "Memories of a Former Kid," by Bob Artley. Some she glued into scrapbooks. Later, she just tucked them into the pages. Did she want to reread them someday? Or did she know that years later her children would find them and chuckle?

Humor surrounded us back then. Every evening all three television networks offered comedy. "Jack Benny." "The Monkees." "I Love Lucy." "Happy Days." "Rowen and Martin's Laugh-In". "All in the Family." How many more can you remember? Laughter filled the living room nearly every time we turned on the tube.

Modern research has proven the positives of laughter. It relieves stress, stimulates the heart and lungs, strengthens the immune system and can even lessen pain. When we laugh, our brains release endorphins; we relax and feel happy. A belly shaking session of unchecked chortling can even benefit blood pressure and increase our self-esteem.

Did our parents' generation know the many merits of laughter? I think they knew it was good. I think they experienced the happiness it gave them in life.

Today, family and friends tell me that TV comedy is nearly non-existent. I can't help but wonder why. In my opinion, we need to laugh now more than ever.

A few years ago, an elderly gentleman visited the Missouri Valley library every week. He returned one book and checked out one book. Then he made a point to talk to each library worker. As he stopped before me, I smiled, for I knew what was coming. "DeAnn, I have a joke for you..."

What better gift than to make someone laugh? Yes, Jim knew how valuable humor is in life. The man knew how to leave a trail. Maybe we need to be like Jim.

Chapter 10

All I Really Need to Know I Learned From...

Our mother loved chickens. She kept them safe and healthy. She smiled as she gathered eggs. Yes, she loved her chickens, but I don't remember that she ever loved A chicken.

Likely, Mom had her reasons, first and foremost: you are setting yourself up for heartbreak. I will never claim my mother's wisdom.

There are three small chicken coops in my backyard, each housing a different group that lives in harmony, mostly. There is the silky house, the old-age pensioners' condo and the layers' shelter and yard.

The girls get along inside and when I let them outside each day, the groups make their separate ways. This worked until a couple months ago. I caught four young layers picking on an older hen in their group. The old girl managed to escape, but I wondered how I could remedy the situation.

Furry Foot (part cochin, with feathers on her legs) solved the problem herself. That night I found her on the roost, snuggled next to the three pensioners. She had moved! From then on, those four hens stuck together. Sometimes one would sidle up next to Furry Foot, as if to let her know she didn't have to stand alone. I called them sisters, though Furry was older. She had hatched ten years ago, and grown up to be a sweet, gentle hen. She raised babies and continued to lay eggs well into her golden years.

Every afternoon this summer the chickens rushed out of their respective condos for their romp in the outside world. Then one night I heard a commotion and found the younger hens attacking Furry again. She didn't run, just hunkered down and tried to hide her head. I rescued her and later found her with her "sisters." This happened a few times and I didn't like it. Research told me that younger chickens will attack an old member of the flock when they sense she is on the verge of death.

A few nights ago, I noticed the old dear didn't roost with the others in their coop. I surmised that she could no longer fly up to the roost. But she found a warm spot in the nest in the corner. The next night, as darkness set in, she waited at the door until I lifted her in.

Yesterday I opened their door and watched as the other three old hens flew out. "Come on, Furry Foot. You can do it!" She stared at the open door for a bit. Then she turned to the corner, sank to the ground, tucked in her head and closed her eyes. My heart hurt for her.

I reached in to pick her up and held her on my lap. I petted her. Told her thank you for being a good chicken. The younger hens were hovering around like vultures. I wondered what I could do to keep her safe and still give her some sort of happiness in her last hours. The garden! I opened the gate and set her down. She found a rotten tomato and probably thought she had gone to chicken heaven. Her sisters remained close to her on the other side of the fence. When the others had gone inside, I carried her frail light body to her home, wondering if she would make it through the night. This morning I peeked out the kitchen window. There she was, basking in the sun.

Some people think it is ridiculous to give animals human characteristics (anthropomorphism), but I know more who have loved animals and described them as "just like human."

Yes, loving them sets us up for heartbreak, but think what they add to our lives. Think of the lessons they teach us:

Sometimes we need to get a little help from family and friends.

When our bodies start to fail, we just need to adapt.

Caring hands (and a Walk Through the Garden) can make all the difference.

Chapter 11

Life Lessons from a Lunchbox

Golden leaves crunched under the children's shoes as they trekked the last mile home from country school. At the neighbor's driveway, the little girl waved as her four companions turned toward their house. She couldn't wait to tell Mom about her day, but she didn't dare run, for she carried something wonderful in her lunchbox.

Last night Mom had rinsed a tall, blue canister. "I found the thermos for your lunchbox," Mom had smiled as Deloris dried the shiny metal cup that fit over the top. "You can take milk in it for your lunch."

The girl's nose wrinkled just a bit. She knew the folks made sure Bossy got milked every morning and every evening. She knew that milk helped make strong bones and teeth, but she didn't particularly like milk; she couldn't help thinking it sometimes tasted like...grass.

Twisting the dishtowel inside the thermos, Deloris had noticed that the lining was a shiny silver. Then she thought of other wonderful things that the thermos could hold. Mom made the best hot cocoa in the world. The girl imagined a tiny wisp of chocolate-flavored steam rising as she poured the sweet liquid into the metal cup. Or maybe on a frigid winter day, Mom could send a thermos of vegetable beef soup. It would help warm her insides even if the stove in the middle of the school room could barely keep up. Yes, it was going to be wonderful to have her own thermos. She gently pushed it into the curved wires that secured it into the top of the metal lunchbox.

The next afternoon, with bag of books over one shoulder and lunchbox in the opposite hand, she again hurried down the hill toward home. Her tummy rumbled. Maybe a stack of cookies would be cooling on the table. The girl grinned as she thought of her little brother gobbling down Mom's soft, chewy molasses cookies. She passed the mailbox and turned into the yard.

Then something dreadful happened. Somehow, her faithful lunchbox with the thermos tucked in the top, crashed to the ground! She quickly reached down, but as she lifted it, she heard an unusual, tinkling sound. The girl plopped onto the grass on the side of the drive and lifted the lid. The precious thermos remained in its holders, but as it rose with the cover, something shifted inside, something that sounded a lot like broken glass. Tears filled her eyes as she realized all those cozy comforts she had dreamed of had just been wrenched away.

She trudged to the front door, dreading the thought of telling her mother. After all, Mom had entrusted her with such a special gift. Mom turned from the stove to greet her child, who normally bounced in, bursting with stories of the day. "What's wrong, Deloris? Did something happen at school?"

Tears pooled again as the girl placed the lunchbox on the table and opened it and lifted out the thermos. The mother's heart hurt, for she could feel her child's pain. She hugged her shoulders. "I didn't even think about the inside being breakable."

Later that night, when the children were tucked in bed, Mom told Dad about the broken thermos. "I shouldn't have sent it with her yet. She is too young." His head tipped and he thought for quite a long time. Finally, he looked up at his dear wife. His eyes glistened.

"You cannot blame yourself for that." He breathed out a heavy sigh. "You know, we can't protect them from getting hurt or having disappointments. How else will they learn that is part of life?"

Mom nodded solemnly, knowing her husband was right. But she silently resolved to be more careful in the future. Dad smiled to reassure her that everything was alright. But, for a long time, on every trip to town he could not help but scan the shelves for a small blue thermos with a shiny metal cup on top.

Deloris with her lunchbox. Thanks to Deloris for the photo!

Chapter 12

The Secrets of Interior Design

Our mom used the seven elements of design in her decorating scheme—Deloris, Donald, Darlene, Dorothy, Delmer, DeAnn and a mother's love. In our farm home special art was positioned with care utilizing just the right space. Walls, lamp tables, the bookcase, china cupboard, and the kitchen table were all prime areas for display.

When one of her children created something, at home or at school, Bible School or 4-H, Mom made sure it held a place of honor in her heart and in our home. She would clutch the work in her hands as though it were made of gold. "Oh, thank you! It's beautiful!"

It didn't matter if the eyes were crooked on the pine cone turkey. Santa's cotton ball beard might have fallen off. We may have colored out of the lines on the small Christmas tree ornament. Mom's praise was unconditional; she understood the need to encourage us. Likely, she remembered her own childhood when approval was sometimes hard-earned. At country school, our mother feared getting a slap with the teacher's ruler if she used her left hand to write or draw.

Deloris spent hours woodburning a detailed picture of a horse and her colt. The next day that piece shined in the light above the buffet in the kitchen.

As we washed dishes, a plaque stood before us, just above the splash board. Alphabet macaroni in a not-so-perfect pattern spelled out the words of a kitchen prayer.

"God bless my little kitchen.
I love its every nook.
And bless me as I do my work,
Wash pots and pans and cook.
And may the meals that I prepare
Be seasoned from above
With thy great Blessings
And thy grace,
But most of all thy love."

Deloris recalls the piece of plywood on the table and bowls of alphabet macaroni spread out for sorting. She, Donald, Darlene and Dorothy spelled out the words and glued the tiny letters onto the board. Mom was so pleased she had them make two more kitchen plaques for her sisters, Julia and Lilly. Mom must have figured they needed help with their interior design since they didn't have their own little elements to decorate their walls.

One year, the girls in Deloris' 4-H club made tablecloths and stenciled on leaf patterns. Mom carefully stored that cloth and brought it out every fall. Another 4-H Christmas project was making whipped candles. As a result, globes of textured white wax enhanced with glitter sparkled from the center of our table that winter and for several winters after.

In Mrs. Sprang's second grade class we made cutting boards to give to our mothers for Christmas. We sanded pine boards, stenciled them with red snowflakes and varnished them. Mom saved hers for holidays when it served as a base for hot casseroles. Never did a knife touch that board. I know because it now graces my cupboard.

I do not remember ever browsing the aisles of the interior design departments in city stores. We never paged through the home art section of the Sears catalog. We all thought Mom's decorating style worked just fine.

It is said that beauty lies in the eyes of the beholder. Our beholder thought everything we made was beautiful. And that was all that mattered.

Chapter 13

Just Like Christmas!

I stomped the snow off my boots and opened the door to the kitchen. "Mom, I got the mail. Looks like we got nine Christmas cards!" Mom's face lit with a smile as she took the bundle from me.

Every year, beginning the first of December, Mom took time each night to write Christmas letters. She had a long list and began with those who lived far away. Cousins in Sweden and Minnesota. Friends and relatives in North Dakota. With boxes of cards at her side and a thick tablet of lined writing paper on her lap, she penned a personal letter to each person. She updated them on the family, the weather and harvest for the year. Recalling their letter from last Christmas, Mom inquired about health and children. She filled both sides of at least two sheets, folded them neatly and tucked them into one of the Christmas cards she had chosen. Family and friends who lived close by only needed one page of news and greeting, but she still wrote something. Dad also had a part, writing his own letters to his brothers, nephews and nieces on the east and the west coasts.

Every morning someone ferried the folks' stack out to the box at the end of the drive. Later, the metal mailbox door clunked shut, and our trusty mail carrier drove off, carrying our cards a step closer to their destinations and leaving our loot.

Getting a whole stack of cards was "just like Christmas!" Mother would place them on the kitchen table until she had a few moments. Then she would slit each envelope with the opener and one by one, relish those letters. Sometimes I sat next to her and she would set the opened cards in front of me. I felt pretty important as I unfolded those pages of words and tried to decipher the sometimes-scribbly handwriting.

The opened letters waited near Dad's place at the table. While Mom prepared noon dinner, he read through them. While they ate, they talked about the Christmas letter news. They would remember to pass it along to their siblings or the neighbors, who would be glad to know.

If mom had saved those letters every year (which she did), the annual installments recorded family histories. The marriages, new babies, years of college or military service, more marriages and grandchildren. Mixed with the joys came the news of tragedy—the tornado, the fire, the cancer. But the letters kept coming like heralds of hope and signs of faith in the future.

Those years of growing up on the farm were prime time for sending letters and cards. The cost of long-distance phone calls added up quickly. In contrast, postage was not terribly high, and beautiful cards were available at about every retail store, at pennies a piece. Handwritten messages tucked into the cards told stories, communicated thoughtful concern and wished happiness to the receiver.

The first Christmas card came about in England in 1843.

Henry Cole (who conveniently worked for the post office of that time) hired John Horsley to paint a holiday picture. Mr. Cole printed up a batch and sent them out. The cards as we know them did not take off until 1915 when Hallmark marketed them in quantity.

Today e-cards and text messages often replace those annual handwritten family journals. Isn't it ironic how we have more labor-saving devices than ever, but find it harder to take the time for the little things?

The first of December I still hurry to my mailbox in anticipation. I think of Mom and Dad and how they enjoyed those annual accounts of family and friends. They never complained about writing them; it was a tradition, a small way to show the Christmas spirit. And they loved getting them. Today if there is a card or two in my mail I smile as I stomp the snow off my boots and head to the kitchen table to enjoy them—just like Christmas!

Christmas card from years ago. Thank you, Susan!

Chapter 14

Dear Santa, Delmer Ate Your Cookies!

"How much longer 'til Christmas?" Mom likely grew tired of my incessant question; it seemed to me like Christmas would NEVER come!

"It's only two weeks away," she replied patiently, then attempted a subtle diversion. "Why don't you bring up a jar of applesauce for supper?"

I headed to the porch on the way to the basement. Visions of Christmas danced in my head, so I was startled to see movement ahead of me and hear the freezer clunk shut. The typical Delmer grin, decorated with sparkling braces, greeted me. Was there a glaze of guilt? I saw him reach for two chocolate chip cookies he had pilfered from the metal canister in the freezer.

"I'm gonna tell!" I threatened my mostly OK brother.

"Go ahead. Mom won't care."

Since early December, our family had begun preparing for Christmas. We had baked the first batches of cookies to be stashed for company, gifts and other gatherings of the season.

Mom hummed hymns as her daughters gathered 'round to

help. Swedish kringlers and spritz, thumbprint and chocolate chip cookies began filling the pantry and freezer. We baked cut-out cookies in tree and star shapes. Mom perfected her own melt-in-your-mouth sugar cookies. We flattened them with a glass and sprinkled on red and green sugar.

Our mother and her sisters were all excellent bakers and we relished their specialties at family gatherings. Aunt Ida made delectable date pinwheels. Aunt Julia shared her famous molasses cookies. Her recipe had appeared in the Christmas recipe section of the Watertown paper. Probably at the same time we were baking, our aunts were also garnering goodies.

In my childhood innocence and adult ignorance, I have always just assumed that cookies have been around forever. Truly, I can picture the young boy Jesus coming home from a long day at the temple or in Dad's shop. "Thanks, Mom, for the cookies and goat's milk."

Lo and behold, I learned that the culinary confections came about much later. In 1796, what is considered the first American cookbook was printed. In it was a recipe called "Christmas cookery." The author, Amelia Simmons, warned that the cookies would be hard and dry at first and should be stored in an earthenware pot in a cellar for a few months. Cookies were a relatively new idea, invented for long-term storage. The typical cakes and pies of long ago became rather furry when kept for company, but those hard, dry cookie concoctions could be made in copious quantities and kept for prolonged periods.

But centuries later, when we looked forward to Christmas on our South Dakota farm, the cookies were not hard or dry. As for long storage, well, obviously those early settlers didn't have Delmers. No way would cookies last for months!

But some must have survived the freezer raids that year and

Christmas Eve finally arrived. I asked Mom if we could put out a plate of cookies for Santa. She nodded indulgently to her youngest child and headed for the freezer.

"Hmmm. Looks like some cookies are missing." My eyes flew to my mother's. Did she suspect the cookie thief? Was she angry? I saw twinkling blue eyes and a knowing smile.

I placed five chocolate chip cookies on one of Mom's pretty plates. She didn't think the reindeer needed any.

The next morning, I dashed downstairs. It was Christmas Day, my favorite day of the year! I searched the table for the plate of Santa cookies. It was empty. Mom read my mind. "Santa must have found them."

But before she turned away, I saw her twinkling blue eyes and that same knowing smile.

Aunt Julia's Ginger Snaps

1 cup sugar

¾ cup shortening

2 eggs (save 1 white to dip cookies in)

½ cup light molasses

2 cups flour

½ tsp. salt

1 tsp each, cinnamon and ginger

2 tsp. soda

Cream shortening and sugar. Add eggs and mix well. Add molasses, flour and spices. Refrigerate. Form into small balls and dip in egg white and into sugar. Space on cookie sheet to allow for spreading.

Bake at 375 degrees until brown and flat with cracks on top.

Chapter 15

Wrapping It All Up

At last, they had made it! The three brushed the layer of dust from their fine robes and opened their travel bags. Caspar removed a shiny piece of gold. Melchior found the bundle of frankincense. Balthazar brought out the bag of myrrh. Their hearts pounded in anticipation as they gazed up at the brilliant star that had guided them, for they knew they were about to pay homage to the greatest King in all of history. Offerings cradled in outstretched hands, the men entered the primitive shelter and bowed before the young child and His parents.

Two thousand years later many people carry on the tradition begun by the Magi on that very first Christmas. We give presents. Countries and cultures may celebrate the event in different ways. Over time customs changed. New ones were added and continued from generation to generation.

When I was growing up, I loved seeing presents under the tree. Boxes wrapped in pretty paper increased the anticipation. Yes, it was certainly fun to know we'd be receiving gifts, but we also loved the giving part. As soon as we were old enough, we accompanied the folks on shopping trips. Taking great pains to keep our selections secret, we found presents for our siblings. Mom helped us pick out something for Dad, who always said he just needed a pair of socks. Dad sometimes took us shopping to find something special for Mom.

To avoid spoiled surprises we usually wrapped the gifts we bought that very night, taking turns at the kitchen table with printed paper, scissors, tape and curly ribbon. One year I remember using white tissue paper; it took several sheets and each present looked like a pillow with a ribbon tied around it.

Delmer didn't go for the gift-wrapping thing, so he often coerced his younger sister to wrap for him. Well—that's another story!

As gifts accumulated under the tree, Mom sternly ordered, "No snooping!" So, we made sure we placed each present back exactly as we found it—of course when no one was looking!

Today pretty gift bags eliminate the need for wrapping. They also make snooping much simpler.

In my research I learned that psychologists claim wrapping presents makes us happy. The best thing to do if we are feeling like Scrooge? Get out the wrapping paper! Then watch the face of the person as she or he unwraps your gift. The "Bah Humbug!" magically morphs to "God bless us, every one!"

I doubt if the gifts of the Magi were wrapped. On cards, they are pictured in small treasure chests. There was no need to keep them a secret, for they were the only gifts and they were wonderfully special in their own right.

Some say the season has become too commercialized. Some say we have lost the true meaning intended by the gifts of the wise men. But I know that hearts still pound in anticipation, for there is joy is the giving and the receiving. And I see peace in the eyes of those who know the One True Gift.

I guess it all depends on how we wrap it all up!

Chapter 16

What Do You Say?

"Hey, Buddy, what do you say?" My heart smiles every time I hear this or a similar phrase from a parent who is teaching his or her child good manners.

My siblings and I may have been young enough to hide behind Mom's apron, but we were expected to say "please" or "thank you" when the situation called for it. I remember one time at a community Christmas event, a Santa was handing out random gifts to every child. He gave me a Little Golden Book that I already had. I WANTED to say, "Could I please have the slinky instead?" but I knew Mom would not appreciate ungratefulness, so I grudgingly murmured, "thank you."

Saying "please" and "thank you," as well as many other actions, were considered common courtesy when we were growing up. We were taught to hold doors open and allow others to get in line before us, especially if they were older.

Someone lugging bags or heavy boxes? It didn't matter if it was Mom, Dad, sister or a potential axe murderer, we pitched in to help, or at least offered.

Whether we were sitting around the kitchen table or having dinner at the annual REA meeting, we would not even think about second helpings until the serving bowl had gone all around the table, or every person in the auditorium had gone through the line.

When Mom started clearing the table, the girls helped. No phone calls or television until the dishes were washed, dried and put away. When Dad did chores, his sons worked alongside him hauling five-gallon pails of feed or filling water buckets at the pump.

Men shook hands in greeting. They removed hats in church and homes. A motherly or wifely elbow in the ribs reminded them if they forgot. There was an overall attitude of respect.

It was OK to tell Mom privately, "I got 100% on my spelling test." But NEVER should we brag about anything to others. When someone was speaking, we did not interrupt. It was not polite to talk with food in our mouth.

If we received a gift in the mail, even a dollar bill or a pretty hanky, we wrote and mailed a Mom-approved thank you note. It was important to show appreciation. We did it and assumed everyone else did, too.

Today, it seems like fewer thank you notes are sent. Even texts and emails have become less frequent for acknowledging gifts. Times change. Habits change. Styles change. Do rules of etiquette also become outmoded in modern society?

Though I realize one can find pros and cons for about anything on the internet, I decided to find out if Emily Post has been replaced. Sure enough, there are a couple of sites that claim written notes are no longer necessary. "People have a lot more things going on these days." "There is not time to find a note, handwrite a message, address the envelope and affix a stamp." One Thank You Note Challenger questioned if people even had stamps these days! She contended that written notes went out with jean jackets.

But there were many more posts that expounded the value of showing gratitude by writing a note, that receiving a thank you card is more meaningful now than ever. Psychologists cited studies proving that expressing gratitude improves mental and physical health. When we put thankfulness into words, our attitude shifts to positive thoughts. Immune systems are strengthened. High blood pressure numbers drop. In a nutshell, sincerely saying "thank you" makes us happy!

Gratitude is more than a response; it is an attitude. Manners are defined as "a sensitive awareness to the feelings of others." Together they affect how we communicate. How we communicate shapes our relationships.

Should we allow the "old-fashioned" practices of good manners and gratitude to fade away into our modern, hectic society?

Our choices make a difference. We can still choose to practice gratitude. We can still choose to be thoughtful of others.

As my youngest daughter recently stated, "Everything comes back into style eventually."

I do still wear my jean jacket.

Chapter 17

Twelve Chapters, 365 Pages

"A new year is like a blank book, it has 12 chapters and 365 pages, and you are the author. My wish for you is that this year you write the most beautiful story possible for yourself."

I received this text from a daughter on New Year's Eve and decided to share it with readers all across the country. Though we do not always have control of the total plot—what is dealt to us—our story is written by how we handle what we are given and those who walk with us on the journey.

On this New Year's Day, I implore you to tell your stories and encourage loved ones to tell you theirs! Please don't say, "I can't write," or "I don't have anything interesting to tell." Every one of us has inspiring, scary, funny, unbelievable, to-be-treasured times in our lives that need to be shared.

Struggles? Have you dealt with cancer or some other dreaded disease? Are you a survivor? Was your heart torn apart from the loss of someone you loved more than life? Tell about the difficult times. You might change a life! You never know when your story might help others overcome obstacles in their lives.

You might impel them to face their struggles and keep going.

The younger generations need to know that life was different when their parents and grandparents grew up. Ok, maybe we didn't walk ten miles to school every day, uphill both ways. But we didn't have cell phones. Some didn't have television or even electricity. Imagine that! Without modern-day conveniences, people had to work harder in harsher conditions. On the farm, tractor cabs were not heated or air-conditioned. Before that, there were not tractor cabs! Before that, there were no tractors! A bucket of water and measure of corn and oats fueled Ol' Dan and Toby to pull the single blade plow ten more rounds.

Likely, many cannot even imagine learning to drive with a manual transmission! I think every youngster should experience the frustration of "killing the engine" (lurch, lurch, silence, bad word...) after letting up the clutch too fast.

Tell of the happy times, the traditions, the people or pets, whether family, friends or total strangers who impacted a moment, hour or months of your life. Tell the funny parts, for laughter joins generations. Laughter and memories help us through the ups and downs of life.

Tell of your birth, your parents and siblings. Tell of love and loss. Tell about the things you ate and the toys you played with.

When we die, our unique part of history is lost—unless we tell our stories. Write them down if you can. Record them or ask someone else to preserve them in some way. But no matter what, tell them. Our tales are a legacy. They leave a trail, a gift to future generations.

I remember our parents voicing how fortunate they were compared to the way their folks had lived. My generation probably feels the same. ("Kids have it easy these days!")

In 70 years will that generation also feel that they had it

tougher than the youngsters of their day? Only time will tell—well, time AND our stories!

Chapter 18

Words We Never Used

I was flabbergasted at a recent post on social media that listed words that have fallen out of use over time. This awakened childhood memories. Yessirree, Bob! Dad often made it clear that we never wanted to act like certain nincompoops who were always pulling stupid shenanigans!

All that remembering made me think of words I often hear these days that we NEVER said when we were growing up—"I'm bored."

Maybe those words were not in vogue then. Or maybe we ventured to say them once. Dad's likely response: "Well, the chicken coop needs to be cleaned. Delmer will pull the manure spreader right up to the door. You skedaddle now!"

But, no fooling, I truly believe we never said those words because we were never bored. There was always something to do, something to see or someplace to go. Whatever the weather, the outdoors was our playground. A trek through the shelterbelt proffered nature at its finest. Currier and Ives landscape and wildlife scenes awaited us; we only needed to look. Each season offered new beauty and wonder. Squirrels, rabbits, deer and pheasants scurried through the trees. We learned to follow tracks without a guidebook.

There was always something to see in pastures and barns. We could snuggle kittens, scratch a gentle sow's head, pet a young sheep or watch calves frolic in the grass. If we were lucky, we might find little banty's secret nest. In winter months, cows played king-of-the-mountain on the snow piles.

Is it just me, or did we get a lot more snow back then? Our sleds scooted down hills and snow piles. We figured Dad used the loader to build our personal Mount Everest. Once the ice was solid, we stepped into our long-johns, threw our ice skates over our shoulder and headed for a frozen pond or the stock dam. One thing that never came out of our mother's mouth: "You need to stay inside. It's just too cold out there."

Over Christmas break I remember a couple nights when Delmer coerced me into playing catch with the football under the yard light. Probably a bribe— "Come on, DeAnn, it'll be fun. I'll teach you to throw a spiral." Or maybe—" Ok, I'll play Skunk later instead of trouncing you at Monopoly." Possibly, the cold, fresh South Dakota air beckoned. Whatever the reason, our boots scrunched over packed snow as we tossed, caught and fetched that pigskin those frosty December nights.

Long winter evenings never seemed long. There were puzzles to put together, games to play and always books to read. Santa or siblings made sure to add to our entertainment stashes every Christmas. We each had our favorites. And the kitchen table proved the perfect place.

No, I do not ever remember being bored. Sixty-some years later, I realize how good we had it and wish for the same wonders for today's youngsters who are so often seen with nose to screen.

The boredom topic was percolating in my brain, so on Christmas Day as my grandson followed me through the new snow to do chores, I asked him, "Jackson, do you ever get bored?"

The nine-year-old wonder looked up at me like I had slipped a cog. "No, Grandma. There are so many cool things to do. I never get bored!"

Suddenly, the world does not seem so discombobulated.

Chapter 19

The Excitement and the Danger

"Ha! Ha! I laugh at danger!" Ralph, fearless explorer sets out for the one place he's never been before—the North Pole. In this delightful children's book, *Ralph's Frozen Tale,* the boy loses his sled and his huskies, yet still plods on through the frozen north to his quest. Little does he know that a great big loveable polar bear is watching.

Though some may compare South Dakota winters to living at the North Pole, as kids we saw the deep snows of winter as wonderful opportunities for excitement.

Every blizzard meant clearing the yard of the sparkling drifts that settled in around the Quonset, barns and chicken coop. In January Dad and Don managed to build a Mount Everest off the beaten path, but in clear view of the kitchen window. Dragging the sled or a big piece of cardboard behind us, we trudged up the side of the mountain. At the top, we scoped the path that would take us on the longest trail, hopped on the sled and leaned forward. Wind in our faces, we squealed in delight as we careened down. The sled had a mind of its own, so we might glide to a gentle stop in front of the barn or crash into the stack of straw bales. Always, the goal was to break the record of the previous ride, whether it was our own or a sibling's. Always, we climbed again for another daring descent.

Delmer saw the snow mountain as more than a sled trail. He used Dad's big aluminum scoop shovel to a carve a hole in the back side, then hollowed out a space just big enough to crawl in. In spite of sitting in snow, he reveled in the quiet warmth of his snow cave as well as avoiding his pesky little sister. Likely Dad monitored his son's architectural feat, gauging the danger of an avalanche or cave-in. Likely his thoughts drifted back to his own childhood on the farm.

The folks seemed to understand the need for fun in life, though I think the intensity of Mom's prayers increased to record highs when she saw Dad hitch the "tin" to the John Deere 520 tractor. The makeshift sled was a rather wrinkled sheet of metal. Front corners bent in jagged peaks, formed by icy treks to the cattle yard laden with alfalfa bales.

"Hop on!" Our father's eyes twinkled as we clambered onto the back, excited for the adventure and just a little bit scared. The boys tried standing, as though issuing a challenge to be toppled. I snuggled in between Deloris, Darlene and Dorothy. Dad put the tractor in gear and gently pushed the clutch forward. He started out slow, keeping an eye on the riders as he circled around the buildings. We all wore victory grins until the driver headed to open ground. A fast curve had both boys sprawled in a snowdrift, howling with laughter.

We girls waited in anticipation, unsure if we wanted to cling to the safety of the sled or experience the wild flight into a bed of snow. Dad grinned and pushed the throttle forward. After the final uphill curve our coats and mittens were caked with snow and the tin was empty.

We crawled back on in tired contentment, thoroughly excited about our arctic adventure, but secure in our safety.

Today, after extensive study, psychologists contend that risks are necessary for children's growth and development, that guided risks help kids learn to manage risk intelligently.

Strange, isn't it? Parents back then seemed to understand that balance of child-rearing techniques. Some fun. Some danger. Lots of learning. Mistakes. Consequences. Rewards.

They didn't need a psychology book. They had frigid, snowy Midwest winters!

Grandsons with double runner sled

Chapter 20

Spring Hopes Eternal!

"Winter storm warning...windchill advisory...winds up to 45 mph..." My weather radio drones on with foreboding forecasts of the arctic blast to come.

Growing up on our South Dakota farm, I don't remember the folks complaining about the snow or cold, and there was plenty of that back then! We took winter in stride and dealt with it the best we could. Dad and the boys made sure the water was not frozen in the livestock tank. "The tank heater may not be able to keep up," Dad said as the three headed out into the blustery wind. He added, "When you feed the cattle, be sure and check on that cow that will be calving early."

Mom and the girls helped where we could. A big teakettle always steamed gently on the back burner of the cook stove. Hot drinks and warm-from-the-oven cinnamon rolls fueled the farmers for their next snowy trek. Mom bundled up and trudged to the hen house several times a day. On the coldest days, the eggs might freeze in the nests. On those rare occasions, she set the cracked white treasure in a custard cup to thaw. We certainly could not waste it!

At the time, I did not realize it, but nestled into those cold winter days were subtle signs of spring. There was the seed testing. Delmer brought in a coffee can of oats from the granary. He laid out ten rows of ten oat kernels on a piece of old towel, carefully rolled it up, wet it under the faucet and set it in a pan on the cookstove reservoir. In a few days he would unroll that cloth to see how many seeds had sprouted white roots. A report to Dad on the rate of germination determined the drill settings for spring planting.

Mom spent evenings poring over her mail-order Gurney's catalog. Choices made, she carefully printed numbers and names onto the order form. Her check and order went with the mailman in the next day's mail. In a few weeks, a leaf-printed box would arrive. Later, when the time was right, we nestled seeds into soft black earth. Each tiny seed was planted with hope—that it would sprout and grow, that it would give us food for body and soul.

Though the evergreens outside my window today are flocked with whiteness and the bare birch branches snuggle under a blanket of fluff, there are a myriad of cozy reminders that winter is waning: Each day gives us a few more moments of light. The sun works with a passion melting snow on dark-colored places.

Every night I pore over my garden catalogs, circling old favs and new possibilities. On the counter, two sweet potatoes are soaking in warm water, hopefully to produce sprouts for planting in May.

Outside, nature gifts us with her own hopefulness. The finches at my feeder flash a bit more yellow every day. Squirrels frolic in tree tops. Goldie, my buff Orpington hen has decided she wants to become a mother. (Considering she is about as old as Sarai in the Bible, this is a miracle in itself!)

My favorite signs of hope are the buds that have formed on the trees. There are soft, white fruit buds protruding from the tips of apple branches. The ends of plum and gooseberry branches sport pinkish buds that offer hope for summer bounty. Round reddish clusters shine through bare maple twigs, promising a profusion of glorious leaves to come.

Nature fairly glows with hope—her faith in the future. All around us we can see signs of the coming spring. We only need to look.

Chapter 21

Reinventing the Spool

The wind whispered outside the kitchen window as it carved a new signature into the gentle peaks next to the house. Tomorrow would mean shoveling out in the farm yard, but tonight we were safe and warm inside.

Delmer was on a mission, searching through a drawer. "DeAnn, come help me with this. Donald showed me how to make something really cool." He filched a wooden spool from Mom's stash. "Hey, find me a rubber band."

I grabbed the flat jar in which they were stored and plunked it on the table.

"Thanks. Yeah, one of them should work." Delmer added a thumbtack and a stack of stick matches to the array. He used his jack knife to make tiny notches on the end ridges of the spool. "Gotta have traction."

I got caught up in my brother's excitement as I parked next to him. He carefully sliced off the burny parts of the matches. He dug in the jar for a wide rubber band and threaded it through the hole in the spool.

"You have to fasten it on one side." He angled the thumbtack point into the loop as it peeked out and firmly stuck the tack in next to the hole. He dangled the spool in the air, grasping the open curve of the rubber band. "Now, we have to wind it around the match."

One end of the match protruded next to the flat side of the spool. Delmer used his right index finger to turn the square-sided stick as he held the spool with his left hand. He wound it around and around like the minute hand on a clock. The rubber band tightened. At last, he sucked in a deep breath. "Let's try it."

Holding it with both hands, he slowly lowered the wheely-deal to the table, held onto it a second, then lifted both hands at once. The spool lurched forward. The matchstick flipped to the back but dragged along behind. The contraption traveled about ten inches, then stopped. "Oooh Hoo! It works!" My brother's silver-capped smile flashed. He wound it up again.

About this time, I decided I needed one of these gadgets, too. I found a smaller spool. Delmer helped notch the ends. It took a while to find a rubber band that didn't bunch up at the windy end, but finally one endured the twisting around the match. Show time! Much to my little-sister dismay, mine only traveled six inches.

"Let's try racing them!" Delmer held his at one end of the table and nodded where I should put mine.

I tasted a few agonies of defeat, then proposed a head start. I smirked and lined my little spooly-car up to the center line of the table, where the extra leaf went in for company. "No fair!" my brother moaned, as my car took off for the win.

We tried threading two spools together right next to each other to make a roller-car. We experimented with longer and shorter rubber bands. Squinting eyes tightly shut and holding our breaths, we tried winding the stick tighter and tighter. At the time, we had no idea we were applying basic principles of science. We didn't realize we were creating an invention that was a combination of simple machines.

No, on that wintery night long ago a boy and his little sister just thought we had made something really cool.

Chapter 22

The Way We Were Raised

There it was! —the loose white thread in the corner. A Rrriiipp resounded through the garage as I tugged the string. Just like that, the fifty-pound bag of chicken feed gaped open, ready for scooping. A zig-zaggy length of flimsy string dangled from my right hand.

All at once, a long-ago picture flashed into my mind: I saw Mom's adept fingers searching for the unbound end. She spotted it and quickly threaded it through a loop of the thick red thread. "You just have to undo the first few stitches and you can pull them right out. Then we can use the bag again when it is empty."

The musty odor of the burlap bag filled my senses as I stood next to my mother that February day. The sewn-shut sack leaned into the weathered framework of the barn as mom worked on it. In a matter of seconds, the top of the bag sagged open and a zig-zaggy red tie dangled from her hand. My seven-year-old eyes saw Super Mom.

I watched as she undid two buttons on her heavy coat and

tucked the string into her apron pocket. Later in the kitchen I would wind that length of cotton onto the ball we kept in the pencil drawer. I never questioned why we saved string. I just knew it was handy to have around.

We saved paperclips and rubber bands that came with the mail. We saved pins. Mom's pincushion was full of every length and type of pin imaginable. There were some with pearlescent plastic heads that came on corsages. There were short ones with tiny heads that were used in garment packaging. Mom kept ribbons and pieces of lace and ric rac. Every button was removed from worn-out shirts, pajamas, and coats before they went in the rag bag. A stash of buttons was always on hand, ready to replace one we lost from a favorite shirt.

Food containers, paper bags, glass jars, coffee cans, wooden spools and thick cigar boxes were potential resources for work and play, and we used them for both.

We saved, re-used and repurposed everything we could. Nothing was wasted. It didn't matter if a bit of time and effort was involved; it was worth it. After all, a penny saved was a penny earned. It was what we were taught. It was the way we grew up.

Our parents had no other option. They grew up during the Great Depression and then World War II. Money was scarce, so people got by with very little. Later, the war required rationing. Rubber, metals and food were needed for our soldiers. Folks learned to get along without them or grow their own. They raised their children, our parents' generation, to do the same.

Mom and Dad started out with two horses and a single-blade plow. Wooden peach crates and a rocking chair furnished their farm kitchen. When the children came along, we were taught to save and make do with what we had. We didn't question it;

it was the way of life back then and we figured everyone lived that way.

The crinkled string in my hand suddenly whisks my brain back to the garage and the bag of feed. I smile at my memories and tuck the string into my coat pocket. Later I will wind it around my saved ball of string. Why buy string when I have a perfectly good supply in my pencil drawer?

I shake out the plastic sack that I just emptied. I flatten it and place it on top of a growing stack. I will save them—make some into grocery bags. They should not be wasted—Because that's the way I was raised!

Chapter 23

Spring Cleaning, Screening and Gleaning

The house smelled of lemons. Voice and vacuum noise echoed from the living room. Mom and my sisters were spring cleaning—dusting, polishing, vacuuming behind furniture. For some unexplainable reason, I decided it was a good time to head outside.

A rumbling noise echoed from the "new" granary. (It was not really new, but how we differentiated between the two buildings.) The sliding red doors stood half open. As I drew closer, I noticed tiny particles flitting out through the doors and disappearing up into the cool South Dakota air. I peeked around the door into the open center of the building. Dad stood next to a huge wooden box-like machine. His right hand rested on the handle of a scoop shovel. He saw me and smiled; it was all the invitation I needed.

The contraption was painted a maroon color, though it boasted plenty of nicks and scratches. On a metal label attached to one side was the word "Clipper." On the very top an open hopper sort of vibrated, and I could see the mound in it sink and disappear. Dad scooped oats up into the hopper from a pile on the cement floor. The kernels settled like cake batter as the motor on the engine purred and the inside chugged. Soon Dad went to the back side and scooped up a small mountain of green, tan and gray stuff into a big metal bucket. Dust rose as he poured.

He flipped a switch on the machine and walked to the opposite side. The sudden quiet seemed strange. "You can hold the bag open." He pointed to a light brown gunny sack. I opened the top. He used the aluminum shovel to transport millions of bright, golden kernels into the bag. "This is our seed oats," he explained. "We have to clean it to get the weed seeds, husks and dirt out." I felt pretty important. I got to help AND learn a lesson in farming.

Dad flipped the switch back up and the belt on the motor whirred back into motion. Oats and gleanings dropped through the screens and came out in the proper places. After a bit, Dad scooped again. The five-gallon metal bucket stood nearly overflowing with the gleanings. I lifted the handle and looked up. "Want me to haul this to the chickens?"

His eyes twinkled for we both knew I couldn't move that heavy thing two inches! "No, but you can help me." I held onto the handle while he hefted the bucket to companion with the other two along the granary wall. "We'll add it next time we grind feed." I frowned, wondering why we would add garbage to the oats and corn and protein we ran through the mill every week. "Those weed seeds are full of protein and other nutrients. The roughage is good for the animals, too."

The process made perfect sense back then. People grew or produced everything they could. Why buy it if you can raise it yourself? Even grain seed to plant in the fields! Of course, nothing should be wasted, so the gleanings became livestock feed.

When Delmer was old enough, he took on the task of cleaning the seed grain. Oats, barley, and wheat. The old Clipper poured out thousands of bushels of good things.

Years later, the elevator in town did seed cleaning for a small fee. One of the guys took a wagon load in and pulled it back home all cleaned and ready to plant. One bad thing about that: we didn't get the gleanings!

Today as I glance about my living room, I decide I really should pull out furniture and vacuum and dust and polish. Yup, I should do some spring cleaning.

Then I remember heading outside to the dust-clouded granary many years ago. I can't help but smile and think THAT spring cleaning was a lot more fun!

An old grain cleaner at the Harrison County Museum, Missouri Valley, Iowa

Chapter 24

Udderly Irresistible

Sprinkles and Mudcat purred and rubbed against my legs as I sat on the front step. My sisters were inside making supper. Mom and the guys were out doing evening chores. Suddenly both cats lifted their heads and turned to stare at the barn. I saw the side door open, heard my brother call, "C'Boss," and watched our milk cow clamber into the barn. The cats took off like lightning and disappeared into their own barn entrance.

The process of putting milk on the table on our farm was a family affair. Mom or Dad did the morning milking, then let Bossy out to pasture. Late in the afternoon one or two of my sisters hoofed it out to the grassy area on the other side of the crick and brought her home. Donald did the evening milking, but it was Delmer's job to get the feed ready. He measured a coffee can of ground grain into the manger-trough, then topped it with four ears of corn and a small chunk of hay. As soon as Bossy put her head through the stanchions, she sniffed for her feed and reached for it with her long pink tongue.

Donald closed the stanchions so she couldn't back up while

being milked. Then he quickly pushed the "kickers" onto the backs of her long boney legs. These made it difficult to lift her foot in the event that she grew impatient with the person doing the milking or decided she wanted a creamy foot bath.

With the cow in place, my brother reached for the metal milk pail and the wooden stool. He sat on the stool and leaned his head into the soft area in front of her hip. I pictured the scene from just outside the front door, for I had watched it before. Soon I heard the soft clangy beats as the streams of milk hit the bottom of the bucket.

I opened the red wooden door and carefully crept over the tall cement step. If I was quiet, maybe neither Bossy nor Donald would even know I was there. I hoped. I sat on a straw bale a few feet away, partly hidden behind a beam. Two of the cats moseyed over to me, but the one mama cat sat next to the cow, her tail slowly twitching from side to side.

The sound coming from the bucket had changed to a rapid "quish-quish." I imagined the foam rising as the pail filled. The distinct smells of fresh milk and cow's breath filled the room. Bossy's teeth crunched on the hard corn kernels. She tilted her head up and swallowed. Her food disappeared quickly. It went to the first chamber of her stomach. She would bring it up again and do a better job later, for that is what ruminants do.

All at once the mamma kitty sat up straighter. Her head moved slightly and she seemed to be chewing. Then she sat up again. Donald shot another jet of milk right into her mouth. I tried to squelch a giggle, but immediately felt warm wetness hit right between my eyes. I felt it drip down over my face and tried to wipe it off with my hand.

My big brother set the milk pail well out of the way. He undid the kickers and hung them on their nail, then opened the stanchions. Bossy backed out and turned to the door.

Donald poured some of the fresh milk into the pan for the cats. They lapped away happily.

I had to skip to keep up with my brother's long strides as he carried the milk up to the house. I was still a bit miffed at the milk bath and disappointed that my attempted stealth had failed. "I'm gonna tell Mom," I impudently spouted.

Don just snorted and smirked. At five I was pretty naïve, but I figured it out. Mom had also been the recipient of one of my brother's milk baths. And I am pretty sure she just laughed.

Chapter 25

Ruminations: Bovine Beneficence

Every day, late in the afternoon, Deloris, Darlene or Dorothy hoofed it, often barefoot, out to the pasture to get Boss or bossies headed home for the evening milking. My sisters all remember "bringing the cows home" from the pasture. Delmer filled the troughs in the barn with feed. The folks and Donald did the actual milking. There was a time when they milked three cows, which decreased to one by the time I was old enough to toddle into the milking parlor.

Though sweet and creamy, our ruminations of just what happened to the cow's milk once it entered the house are a bit um, skim. Dorothy and Darlene turned the crank on the separator, which used centrifugal force to remove the cream from the milk. Deloris' daily task was to wash the separator. She remembers a distinctive smell, not unpleasant, as she scrubbed. Nothing seems to stir up recollection of what happened after that.

The metal cream cans must have been in the mix. Possibly, during the three-cow dairy operation, there was extra cream and the folks hauled it in the cans to De Smet, though we don't know where. After the Depression and WWII times were still hard. Likely, income from selling cream and other produce helped farmers stay afloat.

Deloris helped churn butter in the small wooden churn as it sat on the kitchen table. Dad loved buttermilk, the by-product of butter making. Mom also used it for baking. Of course, any extra went to the slop bucket, which made the hogs happy. Around that time margarine became very popular. We called it oleo. (Another story?) Though we still enjoyed homemade butter, it gradually separated from our menus.

Mom skimmed the cream off the jars of milk once they sat in the refrigerator for a day. All of us remember enjoying the cream of the crop! Creamy gravy on mashed potatoes. Scalloped potatoes, scalloped cabbage, scalloped corn were all made with heavy cream. Peas, beans, carrots and pretty much every vegetable we raised was served, swimming in whiteness. Dad always said the vitamins were in the juice; add milk or cream and vitamins never tasted so good!

The cream added richness to cakes and frostings. Though it was not pasteurized or homogenized or any other -ized, it whipped wonderfully. Salads were creamy. Jello was dolloped. Cream puffs were filled. Ambrosia—heavenly delight!

Home-raised cream combined with fresh farm eggs to make the best homemade ice cream ever! And we had cookies with that!

One of the best things about growing up on the farm was enjoying its bounty. We never worried about calories or high cholesterol then; the family likely wore them off "putting food on the table." (Cleaning the gutter also helped!)

Do you or your dear ones have memories of milking and what

you did with the milk? De Smet readers, can you fill in the blanks on a possible creamery in De Smet? Or nearby communities? Ethel spoke of the creamery in Missouri Valley in her stories about country school. Was there a similar place in Dunlap? Or Platte? I would love to hear your stories! You can send them to me or see if your local newspaper would like to print them.

Here is an opportunity for you to leave your own trail!

You can also stir up a batch of cream puffs. Fill them with whipped cream and strawberries or whipped cream and lemon curd or whipped cream and vanilla pudding.

Cream Puffs

1 cup water
½ cup butter
1 cup flour
4 eggs

Preheat oven to 400. Bring water and butter to rolling boil. Stir in flour. Over low heat, blend about 1 minute or until mixture turns into a ball. Remove from heat. Beat in eggs, all at once. Continue beating until smooth. Drop dough (about ¼ cup) onto ungreased cookie sheet. Bake 35 to 40 minutes or until golden and puffed. Cool. Cut off tops. Spoon in sweetened whipped cream and your choice of filling. Enjoy and remember...

Our butter churn. Thank you to our niece, Susan, for the photo!

Chapter 26

It's Not Nice to Fool Mother Nature!

"Will you please bring me two sticks of oleo?" Mom asked as she prepared to mix up a batch of chocolate chip cookies. Elbows on the table, I watched her get out her big crockery mixing bowl and long wooden spoon.

"Mom, why don't you make butter anymore?" I thought of the heavenly rich, creamy butter she used to make. The homemade butter was a treat, especially on warm homemade bread. Sometimes she even patted the butter into a special mold to be pretty.

"We don't have a lot of extra cream," Mom replied as she measured brown sugar. "Homemade butter does not keep very long. And I read that oleo may be healthier." As her wooden spoon circled and scraped the bowl, Mom smiled. "Oleo was white at first, not yellow like this."

"How come?" I frowned, for I could not imagine a white butter substitute.

"The dairy farmers didn't like the competition with butter. Oleo was a lot cheaper, but they figured people would not want to buy white margarine. So, the oleo manufacturers tucked in a little capsule of yellow food coloring. If we wanted our margarine to be yellow, we had to mix in that color."

Today, remembering Mom's margarine memories inspired me to research the product. I churned up some pretty rich all-you-ever-wanted-to-know-about-margarine-but-were-afraid-to-ask facts. It all began back in 1869 when Emperor Napoleon III issued a challenge for someone to create a butter substitute from beef tallow for the French armed forces and the lower classes. A man named Mege-Mouries whipped up a product he named oleomargarine. The name is derived from Latin "oleum" which means olive oil and Greek "margarite" meaning pearl. Though the original product did not contain any olive oil, and was not really lustrous, as in "pearl," the name stuck. Unfortunately, Mege's margarine was not savored by the soldiers or the masses. The man sold his patent and the demand for the product gradually spread to America.

The butter industry protested, eventually initiating the 1886 Margarine Act, which imposed fees and regulations against the margarine companies. Some states, Wisconsin in particular, made it illegal to sell yellow margarine. For a time, New Hampshire ruled that oleo had to be colored pink, the idea being that white or pink margarine would not appeal to consumers.

Butter reigned supreme until the Great Depression and the World War II shortages of butter. Margarine was cheaper and companies improved the appearance and taste of the butter substitute. The demand for oleo surged. The stage was set for oleo smuggling. People crossed state lines to where yellow margarine was legal, filled their trunks, and putzed back home. Takes bootlegging to a whole new level!

Not to be out-smeared, manufacturers cleverly bypassed the

"no-yellow-margarine" law by including a small capsule of yellow food coloring with the stark white product. Consumers could squish and mix. Voila! It looked just like butter! (Except for the stripes.)

Eventually the butter wars were put out to pasture. Around 1955, the artificial coloring laws were repealed and yellow margarine could be sold. That is, everywhere but Wisconsin, where using yellow margarine remained a crime until 1967.

For decades the greasy duo ran neck and neck. Television ads persuaded Americans. There were talking tubs and slogans like "It's not nice to fool Mother Nature" and "Everything's better with Blue Bonnet on it!" Do you remember?

The dairy industry refuses to chew the fat. They simply contend: Butter is better.

Chapter 27

The Best Fence

I have one fence. It is three-foot chicken wire attached to steel posts. Its main purpose—to keep the rabbits out of my garden. The fence was a success until July of last year. One industrious bunny found its way inside! Leafy green beans suddenly turned to sad stubs barely poking out of the ground.

Growing up on the farm, I don't ever remember rabbits being a problem; likely Rex handled that. But we had several kinds of fences. A decorative, sort of crimped wire lined the front and side of the house yard. The curved top of the metal fence formed pretty scallops. At the corners it joined woven wire, which completed the enclosure. The fence formed a boundary around the house, clothesline, garden, outhouse and the lawn. Behind the garden was a gate big enough for the tractor and cultivator.

Inside that fence I felt secure and warm, no matter what time of year. It was home. It is believed that childhood memories begin around age four. Must be true because I cannot recall a time when that yard fence ever kept ME in. A sidewalk led from the stoop to the front gate where a curved wire bar fit into a notch, forming the latch. Even small hands could push that bar in, opening to the wondrous world beyond.

A short hike toward the barn, led to another fence that enclosed the barn yard. Two-by-eight boards nailed to thick wooden posts kept livestock in. (Mostly.) I loved this fence. No matter how short I was, I could scope out the scene inside. Knee high to a grasshopper, I peeked between the boards. Later, king of the mountain, I stuck my tongue out at Wooly Bully, my feet on top of the middle board and elbows resting on top. "Nah, nah, nah, boo boo, you can't get me!"

Other times my heart pounded in fear as I heard a horrible crack—a duel between the fence and the mamma cow's head. The boards held fast as Delmer or Donald scrambled over the top in the nick of time.

Around the hog pasture, woven wire kept snoopy flat snouts from entering forbidden territory. A strand of barbed wire ran along the top. Hmmm. Wish I could ask Dad or Don what that was for.

Still another kind of fence girded the pastures and fields—barbed wire. Three or more strands of the prickly stuff kept cattle in or out. It was a challenge to push down on the bottom wire, (between the barbs) and slip between without tearing your shirt. Those with long legs could push down on the top wire and step over.

The barbed wire formed boundaries between fields. Badgers and gophers enjoyed digging in the undisturbed soil. Fence building and repair happened after snow melt, but before planting time. Dad was a stickler for strong corners. He said they were the most important part of the fence. Delmer recalls digging holes with the hand auger, then chopping around the edges to make the hole bigger for the thick railroad ties. Finally, they would tamp around the post to pound the dirt down and hold the corner in place.

Farmers in those days worked hard to build strong fences and keep them in repair. No one wanted to hear the frantic call, "there's a calf out!" which required immediate action, no matter the time of day or the weather conditions.

A rabbit in my garden also requires immediate action, though by the time I see the varmint, he has likely decimated the beans, peas and sweet potatoes. Barbed or woven wire wouldn't keep him out. Certainly not a wood fence or strong corner posts. As I work up a spot for lettuce and spinach, I consider what else I could do to keep rabbits out. Images of Mr. McGregor and Elmer Fudd hop into my mind.

Dad and Dorothy in front of front yard gate and fence. Thank you, Dorothy for the photo.

Chapter 28

No Longer a Requirement

Do you ever realize, mid-stroke, that you have suddenly forgotten an important password? Ever forget a phone number—maybe even your own? Ever notice this happens more than it used to?

How can this be? It cannot be that our brains are aging, therefore not retaining as well as in younger years. Ok, maybe a little of that. We tend to forget things more now because we don't HAVE to remember them. Not long ago, phones didn't store contact numbers. Computers did not ask if you wanted a password saved. We had no choice. We had to remember or suffer the frustration if we did not.

Long ago, in days of old, we were required to memorize. Poems in school. Spelling words. States and capitols. Presidents. Bible verses at Sunday School. The small catechism in confirmation. Speeches for contests. Songs for recitals. We may have groaned a little, but we did it! Some of those tidbits of information remain in our brains, and we are quite pleased with ourselves when we can retrieve them.

I recall our mother reciting for me, verbatim, the very long texts of Lincoln's Gettysburg Address, the preamble to the constitution, Paul Revere's Ride, the Night Before Christmas. Since I was the sixth (the youngest and most spoiled), she either retained information extremely well or practiced between times. A text check with my siblings reveals that she also awed them with her recitation talents.

With all this history of marvelous memorization, why can I not recall an eight-character password? Could it be that my brain has become lackadaisical because it doesn't need to store such information?

A speedy search reveals reality: memorization teaches our brain to remember and prevents cognitive decline. When we memorize, we make our brain stronger and improve its capacity for recollection. Another benefit is improving neural plasticity. Have you ever pulled an old pair of sweat pants out of a drawer and tugged on the waistline elastic only to hear tiny breaking sounds and suddenly realize you won't be sweating in those pants again?

Never fear! Unlike old waistbands, our brains can learn to stretch again. Rote memorization is a great way to strengthen brains. A brain workout benefits our minds as much as a brisk walk, run or bout of weight lifting. Worked muscles results in more efficient function.

The good news is we don't have to cram in a lot of words all at once. A daily dose of memorizing a verse or poem teaches the brain to remember things, to hold onto critical details. It's a challenge worth taking on.

We live in an age when memorization is not a requirement. But doing so provides benefits that are truly worth the effort. Then there is that immense feeling of satisfaction we get when we can whip off that fifteen-line stanza to impress the grandchildren.

It's another means of leaving a trail. We just need to remember to do it!

Chapter 29

Best Seat in the House

The red, white and blue stripes spiraled in circles and disappeared like magic at the top. I stared in wonder at the lighted barber pole on Calumet Avenue that rainy April morning. Dad opened the door next to the pole and followed me inside. The barber looked up, comb in one hand and scissors in the other. "Hello, Harrison. Hello, young lady. You two come in for haircuts?"

"Just DeAnn today. Her mother said it was time." Dad shook hands with the man waiting in one of the chairs and sat next to him. I scrambled up, too, my feet dangling far above the floor.

Outside, the water rushed down the street. Inside the men talked. ".... a million-dollar rain!" The others nodded in agreement at my father's typical assessment and the farmer/barber conversation continued. The crops would get a good start. The price of corn was up. Hopefully it would be even better by harvest. The barber swiveled Haircut Guy to face us as the sound of the electric razor clicked on and buzzed behind him.

"How did your calving go?" One lost a calf in the late March blizzard. The others said they had been lucky this year.

Time passed quickly while the barber barbered and the farmers farmed. At last, the owner looked my way. "Are you ready, young lady?" I slid to the floor as the barber pulled a smooth wooden board from between his cabinets. He laid it over the arms of his chair and pushed it right next to the back. I climbed up on the metal step to the soft leather and finally to the board. I turned around and sat.

Behind me, Mr. Barber stepped on the shiny lever that pumped that chair up and up, an inch at a time. Finally, I was high enough. He flapped open a black cape and tied it around my neck. The cape covered my arms and feet; I imagined sitting on my princess throne.

He twirled the chair to face the mirrors. I saw my reflection, but the items on the counter were far more fascinating. Thin black combs soaked in a tall jar of liquid. I figured it was something to keep the combs clean, but couldn't imagine any germs on combs.

There were big white cups with something solid in them. Brushes with soft-looking rounded bristles stood on their flat bottoms. Three electric razors hung on hooks, cords dangling almost to the floor. There were bottles and jars of stuff that smelled like Dad after he shaved. The barber had just started snipping when the door opened and a man and a boy about my age rushed in.

Everyone said hello. Dad stood and shook hands with both of them. The family was new to town. They asked about area churches. The farmers listed every one. "You'd be welcomed at any of them."

From my princess throne I was watching the boy through the mirror in front of me. Suddenly, our eyes met. He flipped his head and his hair flopped to one side. He didn't smile. I decided he wished he were sitting up here on this board in the barber chair being cool like me.

Soon the door closed behind the two. The barber and farmers stared after them as the street and rain sounds rushed in for just a snippet, then softened. "Nice guy. I hope they stick around."

The chair made a gentle hiss as it slowly lowered again. The barber untied my cape, shook it and grabbed his broom.

"How much do I owe you?" my father asked, though it was always the same.

"Two bits." The barber smiled.

We stepped outside. The barber pole swirled, its light sparkling like diamonds through the rain drops. I reached for Dad's hand. "You were good," he said. I grinned. I didn't tell him I had the best seat in the house.

A newer version of the barber pole

Chapter 30

Curtains and Stars

Curtains...What images open (or flutter) into your mind as you see the word? The curtain in the temple that ripped in two? The heavy velvet drapes in the auditorium that open to the first scene? The frilly lace that covered Mother's kitchen windows?

As with every memory, the pictures that remain in our hearts are our own. They depend on past experiences as well as what is happening in our present lives. Sometimes one memory sheds light on another and the past ushers into our minds like the opening act of a play.

Our Mom had several sets of curtains to adorn the three windows in our kitchen. She would choose the set she wanted, carefully iron the ruffles and panels, then hang them on the freshly washed rods in front of sparkly-clean windows. The kitchen smelled of Tide and sunshine. I remember a pink flowery print valence that practically smiled with cheerfulness.

In my college lit class Dr. Y. postulated on the symbolism of the curtain in our short story: "The reference to a curtain symbolizes a closing." I wondered how he really knew what the writer meant. Maybe Mr. Shakespeare just meant curtain. Fortunately, I kept my mouth shut. I didn't need the final curtain closing my freshman year!

Another set of curtains slides into my memory—the unbleached muslin sheets that improvised as walls in the basement of West Bethany Lutheran Church, rural Erwin, SD. Metal hooks fastened the curtains to some sort of thick rod, wooden or metal, which framed small areas into classrooms. Inside each draped section stood a long wooden table surrounded by metal folding chairs. Likely, the ladies aid had purchased many yards of the tan-speckled cloth, stitched it together, hemmed top and bottom and proudly hung them. Likely, their husbands cut and installed the rods beforehand. Likely, they all felt they were doing their part in furthering children's religious education.

Within those curtained classrooms, my Sunday School instruction ensued. Each year or two, depending on combined grades, I sat within a different curtain with a different teacher and a more advanced lesson book. Usually, the students arrived in our classrooms first. Sometimes we chattered, sometimes we frantically worked to commit the assigned Bible verse to memory.

Our teacher breezed into the room, pulled the curtain shut behind her, and class commenced. Around us, other teachers and kids spoke, but that didn't matter. Our focus centered in that eight by ten-foot room. Attendance charts held first spot in the Sunday agenda. The teacher licked a gold star and placed it in the next box by each of our names. I recall how proud I was when every box was filled; it was important to have a solid line of stars after your name. Then there was the memory chart. We got to lick a red star and stick it on the chart if we could say the Bible Verse by heart. "Someday you will remember these verses when you need them," the teacher encouraged. Thirty minutes of lesson, discussion and prayer before the teacher stood, opened the curtain and we scurried up the steps to our church pews.

Looking back at those Sunday School curtains, I see strength, comfort, and certainty. A caring teacher sat next to us. Soft folds surrounded us. Somehow, we knew something important and meaningful was happening in our lives.

Today West Bethany Lutheran Church rests on a different place, the Ingalls homestead just outside of De Smet. The curtains that I remember hanging in its basement have long ago turned to dust, but the memories remain pressed into the folds of my mind.

West Bethany Lutheran Church, Erwin, South Dakota

Chapter 31

Checking for Miracles

On a balmy February afternoon, I succumbed to the nagging temptation. I could not help myself. Just inside my garden fence I scratched in small patches of seeds—lettuce, spinach and radishes. Common sense told me it was too early to plant, even the tough stuff, but another small voice enticed, "Maybe this year it will stay warm. Wouldn't a salad fresh from the garden be wonderful in March?"

Every day I strolled by that garden spot where tiny seeds waited under a thin blanket of soil. Every day I leaned over the fence to check if by some miracle, they were coming up.

It is said that the apple doesn't fall far from the tree. I am convinced that the need to dig in the dirt, plant things, and watch them grow is a trait either learned or inherited from our parents. I recall following Mom around the yard this time of the year as she searched for signs of new life emerging from the earth. "The peonies are pushing through." She showed me the circle of shoots that looked like a tiny forest of red trees. "Those are tulips." She indicated the pointed green leaves in the front flower bed. We meandered to the sunny side of the yard where several clumps of brown sticks protruded from the black South Dakota soil. Thorns poked out from the woody stems, but Mom's proud smile flashed as she bent over them. "The roses are coming!" At the bottom of those clumps, bright green serrated leaves beamed up at her. I envisioned the perfect red, yellow and white blossoms that would grace our table come July.

Mom wasn't the only one who sought signs of new life every spring. Once the fields were planted, our farmer father needed to make sure those seeds would safely emerge. Mom and we kids never declined his invitation, "Want to take a drive?" A Sunday afternoon or an hour after a thunderstorm provided perfect opportunities to check the crops.

Gravel crunched outside our open windows as Dad slowly putzed around the sections, sometimes stopping for a closer look. Occasionally the right front tire veered perilously close to the ditch. Mom frowned. Dad grinned. "Good stand of oats," he noted as we gazed at the soft green carpet on the right. Farther down the road tiny spots of green poked out of the ground in perfect diagonals. Our father took pride in those flawless rows. "Won't be long and we'll be cultivating." Wire-checked corn allowed cultivation in both directions. Thistles and pigweed didn't stand a chance!

A pair of ring-neck pheasants scurried through the end rows on the field next to the shelterbelt. "They will scratch out some of the plants." Dad shook his head as we all scoped the area for more birds.

Almost always our father's Ford ended up far from our own fields. The neighbor's flax looked good. The rain should make a good first cutting of alfalfa. Baby calves kicked up their hind hooves in pastures. Mama cows gave new babies their daily tongue baths.

Though miles from home, no one minded. There were so many wonders to behold, so many signs of life on those leaving-a-trail Sunday drives.

This year on Good Friday I planted seven hills of Kennebec potatoes (It's tradition!) and a half package of onion sets, though it is still early and pretty cold. Every day I walk by. Are they up yet?

It must be in my roots, for I can't seem to help myself. I need to check for the miracles.

Chapter 32

Hospitality Filtered Through the Ages

The couple made their way through the dry prairie grass from the neighboring wagon. Fina smiled a welcome. "Come sit by the fire. I'll put the coffee on to boil." Thankful she had ground extra beans that morning, she scooped a handful of the course brown bits into the heavy pot. She poured in water from the nearby stream and nestled the pot into the hot ashes of the camp fire. The stack of buffalo chips would smolder for a good long time. In a half hour she used her apron as a pot holder and poured the dark liquid into tin cups for their guests.

Years later, Fina's daughter answered the knock at the door. "Come in! Pull up a chair. I'll put the coffee on." She added a handful of cobs and two sticks of wood to the cook stove. The pump in the corner produced icy cold water to fill the aluminum pot. She scooped in ground coffee from the Hills Brothers can and set the vessel on the front burner. In about twenty-five minutes, steam rose as the woman poured the clear brown liquid into porcelain cups that nestled in delicate saucers on the kitchen table.

Still later in time, our mother greeted company warmly. "It's good to see you. Have a chair and I will start the coffee." She extracted the tall, shiny percolator from its place in the cupboard. She filled it with cold water from the faucet. Nestling the base of the hollow metal stem into the pot, she pressed a paper-like filter into the perforated basket at the top. She scooped coffee in and fit the basket cover over the stem. Finally, she placed the lid on top and plugged the appliance into the outlet above the counter. I watched in awe as water splashed up into the clear glass "hat" on the top. With each rumbly splash, the liquid became darker. In twenty minutes, a red light came on at the base of that percolator. Mom poured coffee into brightly printed ceramic mugs and set them before those gathered around the kitchen table.

Last fall my South Dakota sister greeted me with a hug. "Would you like a cup of coffee? Or there's tea or hot chocolate." I chose a white plastic pod from the little rotating tower and soon the wonderful aroma of coffee and hazelnut filled her kitchen. Within two minutes we sat at the dining room table, happily chatting and sipping from special mugs.

Fond memories of coffee flowed as a result of a text to siblings. They recalled our uncles pouring coffee into saucers to make it just right for slurping. Mom got out her rose-painted cream and sugar bowls and always offered the stir-ins to guests.

Egg coffee was mentioned, associated with coffee at church. Readers, do you have memories to blend in?

Delmer remembers the wonderful aroma of coffee as it brewed. Dorothy perks up with another memory, a blend of smells. Mom kept a couple cans of processed meat in the cupboard for the times when people dropped in unexpectedly close to meal time. As our mother used the tiny key on the can to twist off the metal strip and remove the cover, the scent of Spam filtered into the air and mixed with that of the percolating coffee. Such a memory simmers on the back burner of our brains; at a time like this it flows out and warms our hearts.

Methods of making coffee have changed drastically over the years, but the inborn hospitality remains; we want to share our best with friends and family. So, let's raise our cups! Brew up some of your own memories and share them with someone special. It's a delicious way to leave a trail.

Guests for coffee? Mom always put cream and sugar on the table.

A percolator at the Harrison County Museum. Ours was not rounded at the bottom.

Chapter 33

Sure as the Wind

It stood sixty feet tall. Four sturdy metal legs, anchored to the ground, telescoped to the top where a six-foot wheel of angled blades spun into a blur. The giant sentinel greeted everyone who entered our farm yard—the windmill.

Our memories vary somewhat, but my siblings and I all recall that windmill producing required water for the livestock every day of the year. The turning wheel powered a piston that plunged down 400 feet into the ground and pushed up water, the life force for our cattle, hogs, sheep and chickens.

Though it seemed that the wind did all the work, human management was required. A three-foot wooden handle nestled into one leg of the tower. A heavy wire extended from this handle all the way up to the braking system on the wheel. Lever up, the wheel could spin in the wind and pump water into the wooden tank. Lever down, the wheel was still; the water stopped flowing. The tank under the windmill was the sole source of water for the cattle in the barnyard. If they all got thirsty at once on a hot sunny day, the water dwindled dramatically. "Turn on the windmill," was a common command, though as we got older, we learned to keep an eye on the tank. At about two and a half gallons per minute, it took a while to replenish the supply. Occasionally, we got sidetracked or forgot (or the cows decided to forestall their drinking until evening) and the area next to the tank flooded. Then cloven hooves squelched through a muddy foot bath.

Mom carried buckets to the tank and scooped them full of water to carry to the chicken coop. When new lambs and piglets were to arrive and their mammas waited in the barn, we hauled water to their troughs. Though I did not think about it at the time, that old windmill was about as dependable as you could get.

Research reveals that optimal wind speed for those icons of the prairie was 15-25 miles per hour. I asked Delmer if it ever happened that there was not enough wind to turn the wheel. His reply: "Maybe once or twice. Hardly ever."

When storms were predicted or the South Dakota wind blew at gale force, Dad or Mom or one of the family pulled the wooden lever down to stop the wheel.

Once a year the gear box at the top needed to be oiled. With oil can in his back pocket, Donald climbed the metal footholds that lined one leg of the tower. Occasionally, Dad sent Don or Delmer up the windmill to get a better vantage point of where the cows were in the pasture. With those exceptions, we were instructed at a very young age not to climb the windmill or play around the water tank.

There were a couple summers when bullheads swam the cattle tank. If a fishing trip to Spirit Lake reaped a catch of too-small-to-clean fish, one of the boys tossed them in the tank. It was fun to watch them nose to the top for a fly. One such creature of the deep met its demise when it latched on to the lip of a white-faced cow and hung on. The Herford gave a startled moo and made a mad dash for the pasture.

The memories of the farm that breeze through my mind include the rhythmic clicks that the windmill piston made with each plunge into the earth. The daily sound blended with the calls of the calves, lambs and chickens to create the song of the farm, a gentle reminder that life goes on—sure as the wind.

Only the tower remains—and the memories

Chapter 34

Presents, Pig Farmers and Cookie Jars

There were definitely advantages to being the youngest child, growing up on our South Dakota farm. The biggest one was that by the time they got to number six, the folks had pretty much used up all their strictness. You know the old adage, "Spare the rod and spoil the child." I would have asked, "What is a rod?"

However, there were times when being the youngest was no party. About the time I got all my siblings trained, the oldest ones decided they needed to go off on their own. First college and then all of a sudden, they were about to get married!

So, at a very young age, I found myself sitting next to Mom at my sisters' bridal showers. Our aunts and several neighbor ladies worked together to create quite a production for the bride-to-be. The VFW Hall in Erwin provided the perfect venue. Rows of chairs were lined up in front of several long tables. The bride sat in front, surrounded by her mother, future mother-in-law, bridesmaids and sisters. A mountain of presents waited close by.

Star-studded performances entertained the audience and

honored the bride. Several ladies presented a skit. The extremely talented younger sisters read poems, performed piano solos or sang a solo or duet. Guests wrote words of wisdom or favorite recipes on cards for the bride.

There were games. Mom informed me that if I won, I had to give the prize to the bride. What fun was that? The bride opened the presents on the gift table and the gifts were passed around for the guests to see.

The aunts and neighbor ladies went all out for the lunch, too. Sparkling punch was ladled into dainty glass cups from the punch bowl. One of the aunts poured coffee from the silver service. The women set out snack trays they had brought from home. On each was a slice of rich, fluffy dessert. Bowls of mixed nuts and pastel mints were available for scooping. Happy chatter filled the hall.

Like every tradition, the bridal shower is festooned in history. Just how did all this showering start? There is a story of a beautiful girl in 16th century Holland who fell in love with the miller's son. Her high-society father disapproved of the boy because of his low class. Dad threatened to withhold his daughter's dowry if she did not marry his choice, a wealthy pig farmer. When her friends heard of this, they bought her gifts in lieu of the dowry. The father was so touched by their actions that he agreed to the marriage. It has since been the custom to shower the bride with gifts before her wedding.

Do you have memories of a special event with loved ones? Tell your stories! It is how we leave a trail. Following is my memory:

Years after sitting next to my sisters at their bridal showers the time came for mine. A sister, aunts and neighbors hosted. For part of the program, two nieces stood before us, one holding a pretty glass cookie jar. The other read a poem:

A house should have a cookie jar, and when it's half past three
And Bob hurries home from work as hungry as can be,
There's nothing quite so splendid to fill your hubby up,
As tasty little cookies and coffee in a cup.
It doesn't really matter if .they're boughten or homemade,
Or if they're served with coffee, tea, or lemonade.
Whether they are made with peanut butter, nuts or chocolate pieces.
Just so there are lots and lots for the nephews and the nieces!

Chapter 35

Teach a Kid to Fish and...

It's no big fish tale! If dad even mentioned the words "go fishing," the whole family would be ready and waiting in the car within thirty minutes. Worms dug. Poles packed. Lunch loaded. Tackle tucked in trunk. Even as small fry, we took to angling like a fish takes to water.

As kids we started out with a long, Dad-made wooden pole. Fish line was tied securely at the end. A shiny leader held a medium-sized hook, which was safely stored in the coil of line wrapped around the pole. A red and white bobber nodded at the tip. The pole worked fine as we sat next to the folks. A slimy worm or minnow attached, we dropped that hook into the water next to the boat and waited for a gullible perch, crappie or bullhead. If we were lucky, a few creatures of the deep soon flopped at the bottom of the boat.

Delmer recalls Mom and Dad's early fishing rods. One was black and the other green. They were open-faced reels. You had to rest your thumb gently over the line when you cast. Thumb failure resulted in a tangled web glaring up at the fisherman.

Later, enclosed reels surfaced and soon became standard tackle equipment for our family fishermen.

I wasn't hooked yet; so, when Mom, Dad and Delmer prepared to fish from the shore of Lake Poinsett I explored the beach, climbing on driftwood, and searching for shells. Mom had a bite two seconds after she cast out. She reeled in a perch. The others' bobbers bobbed while Mom brought in the catch. I heard her laugh when Dad gave her the tally. Mom loved to fish.

I was still OK with beach-combing when all of a sudden, my brother gave a wild whoop and a 15" walleye flailed at his feet. He cast again, and the bobber sank instantly. Mom even sat back and enjoyed her son's good luck. There he stood, grin flashing as he geared up for his debut on the next Outdoor Life special.

Not to be outdone, I decided then and there I needed to learn to fish like that. "Dad, will you please teach me to use your spinning reel?"

Dad's eyes twinkled. Visions of broken line and lost leaders danced in his head, but he shouldered the pole and headed down the beach. Delmer let out another gleeful shout. A plate-sized crappie flashed in the sun.

I wondered why Dad was getting so far from the action, but I followed him to a place thirty yards away. He showed me the stop mechanism and how the reel worked. He demonstrated a cast. The leader soared far out over the water, barely making a sound as it broke the surface. He let me reel it in and told me to try.

I lifted the rod. I flicked my wrist. I waited. No splash. The hook, line and sinker had landed in the brush—ten feet behind me! Thank heaven Delmer was too busy reeling in fish to notice.

I finally learned to cast that day. There was a satisfying splash as the worm hit the surface. The bobber rocked on gentle waves. After what seemed like hours, I felt a tug. The bobber went under. "You got one! Reel it in!" Dad cheered. I cranked that little handle for all I was worth. The fish fought. I worried that the pole would snap as I reeled that whopper in. At last, it emerged from the water, floundering on the sand. Dad smiled and reached for the line. "Good job!" he said as he carefully unhooked the four-inch bullhead and dropped it in the catch bucket.

I will always remember that afternoon at Lake Poinsett. I never became a great fisherman like my brother or mother. But I still have stories to tell. And that's another kettle of fish!

Chapter 36

The Best Thing About Fishing

"Wind in the west, fish bite best." The old wives' tale touts wind direction as providing the best times to fish. Famous outdoorsman, Patrick McManus limited the best fishing times to two: "Best times to fish is when it's raining and when it ain't." In our family, Mom and Delmer agreed: the best time to fish is the second you arrive at the lake!

So, one morning in May, after a Dakota deluge, Dad, Mom, Delmer and I trekked the 135 miles northeast to Lake Traverse. Upon arriving, we discovered at the boat rental that the only one available had no motor. Dad stared down at the small vessel floating next to the dock, noting the paddles attached to each side. He glanced up at Mom, who grinned; she was likely imagining all the fish she would haul in. He looked at Delmer. Not many years ago, the boy wanted to fish so badly he toted his wooden pole to the road ditch, where water stood after a storm.

"We'll take it!" Dad paid the man and we loaded our gear into the light craft. The guys pulled in the anchor and Dad paddled out onto the lake. The boat bobbed gently on the waves. A soft breeze floated in from the west. Soon Mom's line plopped into the water, then Delmer's. Dad took in the scenery and eventually cast out on the other side. He looked at me expectantly. I told him I would wait a while. (Mostly, I felt sorry for the worms and minnows.)

Soon fiberglass rods bent and the fishermen reeled in fish. Mom brought in perch. Delmer added bluegill and crappie. Dad pulled in an occasional perch, but kept busy unhooking the catch. Mom laughed as the tally grew. Delmer grinned proudly at the folks' praise. "That's a nice one! It's a three-pounder for sure!" Dad winked at me as he added each to the stringer.

Luck seemed good that warm day as fluffy clouds scudded overhead and the sun sparkled on the emerald surface. But every fisherman knows luck can change in an instant. A sudden gust of wind swept in from the northwest, rocking the boat. The head of a dark cloud appeared far in the west.

"Oooh, I got another one!" Dad watched his son and wife, totally enjoying the moment. There would be plenty of time to row back to the shore.

But the wind had other ideas. A gale charged in, an incessant force that pushed the boat farther from the dock. Dad rowed for all he was worth as the rest of us held on tight, willing the boat to go the opposite direction. A giant wave swept up just as we rocked and splashed a puddle at our feet. Delmer kept staring in the direction we were heading. Rocks and trees jutted from the water's edge. Dad's face was grim as he struggled against the relentless wind. Worry reflected in Mom's blue eyes as she searched the water around us. I was scared. I started thinking we needed a miracle, like when Jesus calmed the water.

For what seemed forever, we kept moving toward the jagged

edge, swept farther and farther from the safety of the sandy beach.

All at once, we heard a noise in the distance. It seemed to be coming closer. Was that a motor? Out of the wild, dark waves a boat appeared. The crew maneuvered close enough to catch the anchor as Dad tossed it over the churning depths. Fighting the wind and waves, they managed to tow our little rowboat back to the safety of the dock.

The next evening, tackle and fish packed in the trunk, the four fishermen headed for home. The driver glanced over at his wife who smiled contentedly. He looked in the mirror. His little girl rested peacefully against the door. He saw his young fisherman son, head leaning back. Even in sleep, his braces sparkled in a happy smile.

Dad's eyes turned back to the road as he sighed a thankful sigh. Yes, he decided, the best thing about fishing is not the fish.

Chapter 37

Getting Our Two Cents Worth

A penny saved is a penny earned...It all adds up...Every little bit helps. They were simple, everyday sayings. They were life philosophies. They were the way we were brought up. So, growing up on our South Dakota farm, when we decided we needed a bit of cash for something special, we went hunting for pop bottles! The grocery stores in Erwin and De Smet paid two cents per bottle.

Early spring made for easier hunting, before the brome in the road ditches grew waist-high. Delmer rode the red Roadmaster. Mine was a smaller version, passed down from my older siblings. If those bicycles had had odometers, they would have racked up thousands of miles over the years! With a gunny sack draped over Delmer's handle bars, we headed down the road.

Eagle eyes scanned the ditches on both sides. Sometimes the clear or green glass sparkled in the sunlight, begging to be found. Sometimes the bottles needed to be rescued from a tuft of last year's grass. A few laid in dirt that had washed from a field in recent thunderstorms. When we spotted one, we pulled off the road, footed down our kickstands and at least one of us descended into the ditch. We took turns unless there were lots to gather.

If Dad had burned the ditch, the pickings were easy to spot. Our shoes may have gotten a little sooty, but we were raking in the dough!

Not all the roads around sections were gravel-coated. Minimum maintenance paths led to the approaches for some of the fields. Down the hill on one particular dirt road, after splashing through two mud puddles, we hit the jackpot—a whole pile of bottles! "Why would anyone throw bottles out here?" I questioned as we carefully added them to the bag. Delmer replied something about parking. I still didn't get it. "Why would anyone park here?" (I was the youngest, most spoiled AND most naïve!)

The gunny sack was getting pretty heavy, but we spotted green glass shining in the ditch at the corner a half mile from home. We were both grabbing bottles when we heard a car approaching. Delmer checked to make sure our bikes were far off the road as the vehicle barreled closer. A couple of teenagers yelled something out the open window. Delmer's fists clenched as he stared up at them. Barely half their size, I know my brother would have fought if he needed to. All of a sudden, a bottle flew out and we jumped out of its path. The car sped off, leaving behind a cloud of dust and an echo of wild laughter.

My brother glared after them. As I happily retrieved the bottle, I placated my brother, "They aren't very smart. How can they throw away good money like that?"

When we got home, we rode straight to the cattle tank. We washed and rinsed those bottles and let them dry in the sun. Next trip to town, we would haul them in and collect the cash.

CHAPTER 37

There were always things to do and lessons to learn when we grew up on the farm. Economics. Old-fashioned values. No matter what, it seems we always got more than our two cents worth!

A Coca Cola bottle on display at the Harrison County Museum

Chapter 38

Just When We Thought It Couldn't Get Any Worse

"I wonder if the northerns will be biting." Delmer could barely contain his excitement. It was a spur-of-the-moment decision. The final field was planted. Corn, oats and wheat seeds were in the ground, waiting to push through the black South Dakota soil. Dad figured this might be the last chance for a fishing trip for a while, and he knew how much his wife and young son loved to fish. The sun was getting low in the horizon as the sparkling waters of Lake Traverse came into view.

The plan was to rent a cabin, enjoy Mom's fried chicken and potato salad, and head out on the lake early in the morning. The problem was, even the best laid plans of fishermen often go awry. There were no cabins available that spring evening. Not one.

Dad drove around until we spotted a picnic table under a gigantic cotton wood, in view of the lake. We spent the night in the car, blankets and pillows tucked around us. It was an adventure; tomorrow we would be catching fish!

But during the night the wind came up. It howled through

the branches above us. It buffeted the Ford. The next morning white caps crashed wildly onto the shore. The guy at the boat rental place shook his head. It was too windy, too dangerous to be out on the lake. Delmer's disappointment reflected in his blue eyes as he looked up at Dad. Had we made the long trip for nothing?

Dad asked around. Were there other places to fish close by?

Well, there was a smaller lake about 50 miles away. It was surrounded by trees.

We headed west through Sisseton, to Nine Mile Lake. In less than an hour, clear blue water came into view. Calm as a clam. Hope lit up in my brother's eyes again.

The old guy in the rundown bait shop smiled as we walked in. Yes, he had a boat we could rent. The water was fine. With any luck, we'd catch something. He led us to the boat tethered to the short dock. "Here ya go." Dad noticed the coffee can under one of the benches. "Oh, that's just for bailing out water. She's got a little leak, but you'll be fine." Boat Guy hurried back to his store. I tightened the strap on my life jacket.

Dad looked relieved when the motor popped to life. Delmer and Mom had their poles ready as we chugged out to the middle of the small lake. "Let's try it here." Our mother seemed to have a knack for catching fish, so Dad shut down the motor and we dropped in our lines.

Sure enough, water soon pooled at our feet. I was thinking maybe I should take swimming lessons when Mom got a bite and reeled in a nice perch. Within minutes Delmer's bobber went under, too. Dad added each to the stringer with a grin.

Since I wasn't catching anything anyway, I decided to start bailing out the water before my red tennies got soaked. It was fun to scoop it up and splash it back out into the lake. "Could you do that a bit more quietly?" my brother asked impatiently. He always was kind of bossy like that.

After two hours the stringer held enough yellow-and-gray-striped fish to fill our cooler and the boat held only an inch or two of water.

On the long drive home from Nine Mile Lake that evening, my brother and I didn't consider the life lessons we had learned on that trip. "Don't give up!" "Try one more time and you will succeed!"

No, as we closed our eyes for the drive-home-nap, we just figured it was all about the cooler full of perch in the trunk.

Chapter 39

They Just Keep Coming Back

Long ago in a faraway land there lived an Empress. One late winter day she strolled through her garden. The bleak, colorless landscape disappointed her deeply, so she issued an imperial decree: "All the flowers in the royal garden must bloom now!" No living thing dared disobey the Empress, for she was known to be ruthless. So, the next day, the imperial garden glowed with orange, yellow, pink and purple. Every flower bloomed in glory—except one.

The woman observed the plant that had dared to defy her. One lowly mound of green stubbornly refused to bloom before its time. Enraged, the Empress banished the plant from her garden. But the next spring it bloomed more beautifully than ever. When she found out, in a fit of anger she ordered the plant with its lovely blossoms to be burned to the ground. At last, the powerful ruler was satisfied that she had destroyed the flower that had not followed her orders.

But the next spring, the plant sprung from the ground and sent up the loveliest profusion of blooms it had ever produced.

Since that time, the persistent flower has spread across the earth and brightened lawns and gardens and tables for another thousand years.

The story is a myth of Empress Wu Zetian who ruled in the Tang Dynasty of China. The strong, stubborn, persistent, yet beautiful plant that defied her was the peony.

In our yard on the farm, two peonies grew on the east side of the house. Every spring, the three-foot mounds produced delicate pink puffs that bobbed in the South Dakota breezes. Closer to the road, a 20-foot row of peonies paralleled the young evergreens and the fence line. These peonies were a deep burgundy, with tiny splashes of yellow protruding from the center.

Neither my siblings nor I know how or when the peonies came to be in our yard. I do know Grandma had several varieties growing in her garden, as well as the aunts. Could be that spring of 1939, after our parents' March wedding, Mom's folks stopped in for a cup of coffee. Selma set a feed sack on the grass. "I brought you some peony roots, the dark red ones that you loved."

Possibly a few years later, Mom's sisters brought a root division or two from their gardens for Mom to add to her collection. Nearly every yard was home to a peony bush. Their lovely scent even greeted visitors to cemeteries when they stopped in late May or early June. Sometimes the heavy blossoms touched the ground, but their pink, white and red flowers offered a lasting tribute to those who had gone before.

I didn't know, and likely didn't care how Mom got all her pretty peony bushes as I skipped alongside her as a little girl. We were going to pick armloads of the silken flowers and I got to help carry them. She would place some in jars of water to take to loved ones' graves at the cemeteries. Some would sparkle in pretty vases to go to a neighbor or a friend. Every year our mother would create an arrangement of peony blossoms and stems of the white spirea that Dad had given her. The bouquet graced our kitchen table until the silky petals began to droop and fall.

As I look back, there are many things I wonder. Many things I wish I would have asked our mother. The wondrous peony plant often outlives humans. When we grew up, they were a common and welcome flower in the landscape. But, how had those steadfast shrubs fared during the Dirty Thirties? Did they doggedly peak through the earth every year, hoping for a few drops of rain to sustain them? Did they send up a tiny shoot which died back in the drought, unable to conceive a flower? I can only imagine.

But I do know that those tough, persistent flora somehow survived and flourished and live on today. How's that for leaving a trail?

Chapter 40

Saving By the Book

It was like a Wish Book. The 170-page catalog revealed pictures of thousands of items, everything from towels and teapots to pianos and cars. A price appeared alongside each item. Unlike a Wish Book, the prices were not listed in money, but in number of books required.

The catalog was called the Ideabook. It was published by Sperry and Hutchinson, a New Jersey based company that offered merchandise redeemable for filled trading stamp books. S & H sold the Green Stamps to retailers who sponsored the trading stamp programs to build customer loyalty. Grocers, gas stations and drug stores offered the trading stamps which were rewarded to their shoppers at the rate of one stamp for every ten cents worth of purchase. The perforated stamps came in values of one, ten and fifty points. Consumers would take their reward stamps home and affix them to the pages of the booklets, which were provided free by the merchant.

Green Stamps were the most popular trading stamps in the United States. S & H began in 1896, but flourished from the

1930s to the 1970s. In 1964 the Ideabook was the largest single publication in the country. It is estimated that 80% of American households collected the stamps during those years and were rewarded with more than 10 billion dollars with of merchandise. Americans were stuck on stamps!

Research revealed the most popular item in the catalog was a toaster. I could not find how many booklets a toaster took, but I did find a plaid plastic thermos cost only one filled book. A fluffy pink bathroom rug set required two and one-fourth books. Fifteen books purchased a girl's bicycle, and 718 stamp-laden books could put a Mustang Hardtop sports car in your garage!

The grocery store in De Smet offered Green Stamps for a time when we were growing up. I remember the cashier first placing the bills and coins of change into Mom's hand after her purchase, then working the Green Stamp dispenser. She pushed down finger slots on a machine to the right of the cash register and detached the stamps that appeared at the bottom. Mom tucked them carefully into her purse.

It was my job to lick and stick the accumulated stamps into the empty booklets. Each page required a total value of 50 points. Most ended up with a full sheet of 20. After licking 24 sheets of stamps, I was wishing for flavored glue! I became very thankful for the bigger value stamps. Only five or, better yet, one of those filled a page! It was fun to stack up the fat books. "What are you going to get with the stamps?" I asked Mom as she did a mental count.

"I have an idea of what I would like to order, but I don't know if we can save up enough books."

My siblings and I all recall the era of Green Stamps and we remember Mom saving them, but only one of us remembered something our mother actually purchased with the stocked-up stamps. A lovely, deluxe baby stroller appeared on Deloris and Lowell's doorstep shortly after the birth of their first child. Mom and the other grandmother pooled Green Stamp books to purchase the special gift which lasted through four more children.

Trading stamps offered a bonus; they helped stretch a family's budget. Shoppers could earn rewards with a little effort and a lot of saving. The stamps reached their peak when those who were kids in the Great Depression grew into adults who could do their own shopping. After years of doing without, it was fun to save up for something special, especially if it was free.

How would shoppers react to trading stamps if businesses offered them today? Would people be willing to save up and take the effort to fill books? Maybe not, but one good thing about it—today we wouldn't have to lick the stamps!

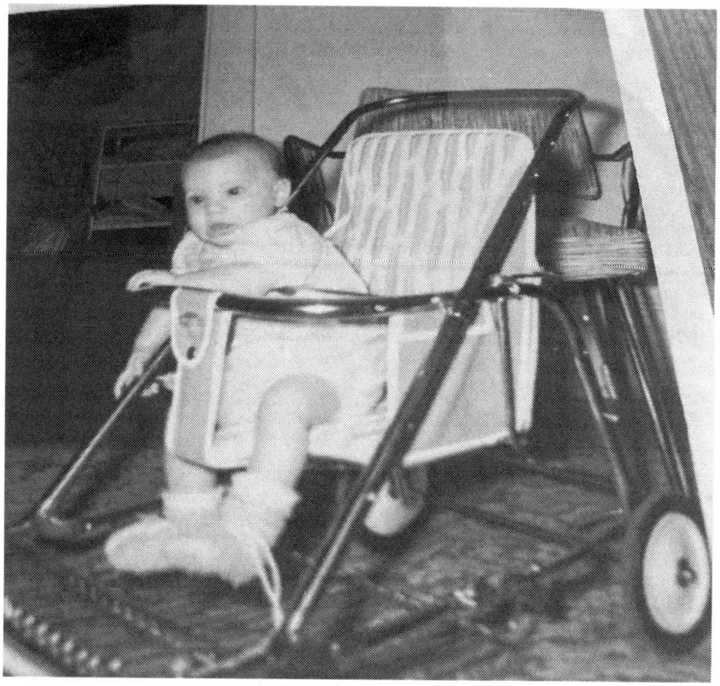

Niece Susan in her stroller from Green Stamps! Thanks to Deloris for photo.

Chapter 41

Sweet Dreams and Sewing Machines

"There's a nice breeze today, good for drying. Let's get the bedding washed." Mom pulled back the blankets on each bed and untucked the sheets, gathering them into a big round bundle. My job was to get the pillow cases. I grabbed the closed end, held it by the corners and jerked up and down until the inside plopped to the floor.

Every pillow I uncovered that day was pretty much the same. Soft and squishy. I picked one up to toss it back on the bed and the top flopped over. Most were encased in heavy fabric of dark blue and white stripes. The pillows on my bed had alternating stripes of light blue and tiny green vines with pink flowers interspersed.

Everyone in our family slept on feather pillows. The pillows were homemade, most likely gifts from Mom's sister. Aunt Julia raised geese, and in those days, nothing was wasted; geese provided much more than Tiny Tim's Christmas dinner!

Only once do I remember Mom making feather pillows. I watched as she sat before her Singer sewing machine. She had bought special fabric for the pillows, pillow ticking. "It's stronger and heaver than regular cotton," she explained as she sewed around the edges of the softly-striped rectangle. She grinned, "We don't want any feathers poking us while we sleep." When she had stitched three sides, she turned the casing right side out and snapped it flat like she did with towels before she hung them on the clothesline. "Come help me fill it with feathers."

Out in the entry that we called a porch, was stashed a stuffed flour sack we had brought home from our last visit at Julia's. I held the empty ticking bag open while Mom scooped in small white feathers and silky down. Tiny parachutes of fluff flew up and around us, tickling our noses and getting stuck in our hair. Mom told me that Julia only used goose feathers; she thought those made the best pillows. Soon the new case held the right amount of feathers. Mom folded the edges in on the feather-filled wrap. "Bring me the pin cushion. I need to pin it shut or we'll have feathers all over the place!"

Mother sewed the end of that pillow shut twice! Guess she didn't want to take any chances of goose feathers taking flight.

Growing up, we took simple feather pillows for granted. Little did we know that in history there slumbers a story of this soft, snooze-time friend. In fact, what ancient societies used for pillows would give us nightmares!

The first pillow likely originated in Mesopotamia around 7,000 B.C. Get this! It was made of stone. It's purpose: to raise the head off the ground so that insects and other critters did not crawl into the slumbering soul's hair, mouth and ears. Those ancient civilizations believed the stone pillow also provided the best support for the head. Memory Foam, beat that! But carved stone was expensive, so only the rich rested on rocks.

A few thousand years later the Ancient Greeks and Romans are believed to have invented filled pillows using wool, straw or feathers, but only the wealthy could afford pillows filled with feathers.

The new inventions vastly improved prospects for sweet dreams. They were also far better for pillow fights.

Not one to let sleeping dogs lie, a foreign inventor came up with the medicinal pillow. This silken headrest encased various herbs and claimed to improve hearing, keep the eyes sharp, return gray hair to original color, regrow lost teeth and cure disease. Where is this pillow when we need it?

A set of feather pillows was Aunt Julia's traditional wedding gift. Only the soft tummy feathers and a few from the back met the Goldilocks standard—just right. No sharp shafts allowed. I could not rest until I found out how many geese it took to provide enough feathers and down to stuff a pillow. More than one source stated that it took 25 to 35 geese to get enough feathers for one pillow.

Still, nothing beats easing one's head into the luxury of a fluffy feather pillow. It's like hugging a cloud, which makes me think I should have hugged Aunt Julia a lot more!

Chapter 42

The Real Taste of Home

Cottonwoods glistened in the sunshine. The unfailing click of the windmill, the mamas calling to their new babies in the pastures and the twitter of a happy robin blended in the gentle South Dakota breezes. Outdoors beckoned. My sisters and I worked alongside our mother as she cooked, cleaned and canned, but when she didn't need us for a bit, we headed out the screen door to our "playhouse" in the trees or the backyard shade.

Thunderstorms sometimes provided our favorite play time ingredient—mud! Our bare toes squished in the black ooze as the earthy aroma rose into the fresh rain-scented air. Splatters that stuck to our bare legs tugged gently at the skin underneath as they dried to gray.

But mud meant more than glorious foot therapy. Mud provided all the basic ingredients for culinary academy: The Joy of Cooking 101.

When Mom could spare Deloris for a few moments, our oldest sister rounded up tin cans and sticks. If there was no

God-made mud, she mixed her own. Likely she had a special recipe for cakes or cookies. Deloris created her own versions of whatever Mom made. The confections baked in the sunshine. Even without cooking spray they popped from the pans, ready for Dad's taste test. Sitting on the front stoop, pinky finger awkwardly raised, he sipped his tea and "nibbled" the sweets. "Delicious!" His hazel eyes sparkled as his little girl glowed with the praise.

Darlene remembers stirring up mud pies in an old pan Mom gave us. The bottom was battered and stained. If we held it up to the sun, we could see a tiny pinpoint of light. Perfect for cooking up wonderful concoctions.

Dorothy used the same pan to mix her secret recipes for pies. She poured the pudding-like batter into small cans. Shredded peony leaves and tiny twigs served as streusel toppings. Even at age four, she had learned from mom that presentation is everything.

As the youngest, most spoiled, I likely had more time to play in the mud than my sisters. I recall filling a quart jar with water which waited on the saw horse that was my table and stove. I filled the hole-in-the-bottom pan with dirt that I scooped from the bare spot next to the sidewalk. I begged an old spoon from Mom and dumped and stirred and added and mixed. There was a soft clay brick that produced tiny orange sprinkles when scraped with a stick. I used the round and oblong tin covers from cocoa and dry mustard for baking dishes. Plastic measures from laundry soap served as tiny kettles or cups, whatever was needed at the moment. A bent nail on the front of the saw horse perfectly adjusted the stove temperature.

Mom always took time to sit and sample and smile. "You will have to give me your recipe."

I wonder if Martha Stewart and Betty Crocker began their cooking careers with the same basic earthy elements. Did their moms and dads sample their creations and encourage them with love? Did they get to partake of that same real taste of home?

Our brother Delmer also got to experience our outdoors gourmet delights. He didn't appreciate our skills quite as much as our parents. "I remember the mud pies and cookies. Sure glad the real ones you made a few years later were better. The first ones tasted like dirt!"

Chapter 43

The Day I Ran Away from Bible School

School was out! I had looked forward to summer for weeks. To ditch Dick and Jane for real books. To follow Mom, and ride the tractor with Dad. Baby kittens needed snuggling. Bare toes longed to touch the leaves high above the tree swing. I couldn't wait!

So, why, on the very first day of summer vacation, was I riding with Delmer, Dorothy and Darlene to the church a few miles up the road? West Bethany Lutheran Church. The cross-crowned steeple atop the white wooden structure spoke its strong, silent message of faith as it stood with its cemetery across the road. Surrounding green fields rippled in the breezes. Every year, dedicated teachers worked together to offer children two weeks of Vacation Bible School.

"Two weeks? All day?" I groaned as the Galaxy 500 rumbled over the gravel.

Delmer popped his baseball into the awaiting glove as he sat next to me. "It's not so bad. We get to do fun stuff."

Dorothy beamed with happiness and clasped her hands. "Oh,

DeAnn, it is so much fun. You get to be with your friends all the time. There's a whole hour for lunch and recess. I love Bible School!"

Darlene, who got to be a helper this year, added her encouragement. "I think you will like it, DeAnn. The teachers are really nice."

The church came into view and Darlene maneuvered the car into an open spot. Everyone piled out quickly except me. I watched some kids play tag. Some swung from the pipe railing that secured the steps. It wasn't long until the bell rang from the tower.

In the sanctuary before us glowed the classic painting of the Good Shepherd, framed with gilded white spires. The white furnishings and red velvet cushions in front of the altar whispered welcome.

The superintendent set forth the daily plans. I heard something about a program and recess and Kool Aid. We sang "Jesus Loves Me" and "Praise Him, Praise Him All Ye Little Children" and worked on a new song.

Finally, we headed to the cool basement where we divided into classes. With curtains for walls, we sat around tables and learned Bible stories. I sat next to friends. We colored, cut and pasted papers to take home. The minty-paste scent filled the room.

At noon we grabbed our lunches and filed outside. I sat with my classmates on the church steps. Birdsong and the scent of lilacs surrounded us. I bit into one of Mom's chocolate chip cookies and was just starting to think maybe these two weeks wouldn't be so bad after all.

The necessary outhouse stood behind the church. There was a boys' side and a girls' side. The weathered door clunked shut behind me. My eyes were adjusting to the semi-darkness when I heard frantic screaming. I rushed out to see what the deal was. A boy held a garter snake by its tail and hooted as terrified girls sprinted away. I felt bad for the snake.

Older boys put an end to the snake incident and a couple teachers came out. "Let's line up and play Red Rover." I grasped the hands of the girls next to me as a boy from the other team charged toward us. I closed my eyes and held on for all I was worth. He was bigger and hit our arms hard. We fell into the grass. My left arm throbbed.

Soon it was the other side's turn. "Red Rover, Red Rover, send DeAnn right over!" Friends encouraged. "Go DeAnn. You can do it." I was scared, but my sore arm sought revenge. I picked the spot I was going to try and break through and plunged forward with all my might. I didn't make it. The kids laughed.

From a young age, our parents taught us to be good sports. You congratulate the winner. You never whine or complain.

I didn't cry. I picked myself up, dusted myself off and started down the road that led to home.

I had barely gone 50 yards when my sister Darlene caught up with me. "Come back, DeAnn, it's time for crafts."

I made it through the remaining two weeks and quite a few years of Bible School after that. Every year I looked forward to summer freedom on the farm, but I never, ever learned to like Red Rover.

Chapter 44

Fit For a King

It was summertime—and the livin' was anything but easy. The farmers needed to cultivate, make hay and harvest. Cattle had to be moved to greener pastures. Plentiful water was crucial, especially when the South Dakota sun beat down with a vengeance. The garden also required constant care. Weeds needed to be pulled. Vegetables had to be harvested and readied for the table or the canner. All the while, we kept a watchful eye for anything that could harm the livestock or plants, ready to attack. Gender roles were pretty specific back then, but Mom still worked alongside Dad in the fields when needed, Dad had no problem lending a hand in the garden or kitchen, and we all pitched in when the situation required. We worked together to put food on the table, literally and figuratively.

It was early July. Rains had brought forth lush green leaves of every variety. The corn was beyond knee-high. Crisp radishes and lettuce salads graced every supper table.

One warm afternoon, Mom sent Delmer and me to the garden on a mission. Delmer carried a tin can with liquid in the bottom.

He swished the can gently. I wrinkled my nose. "It's kerosene," my brother informed me. "It kills bugs."

We headed directly for the potato patch, row upon row of rounded bushy plants with purple and white blossoms just showing on the top. Delmer began scouring every plant. All at once he reached for something on a leaf, and with a look of revulsion threw it into the can. I had to see this thing that was so revolting, so I carefully peered over the side of the can. A round-shaped insect floated on the surface. It was bigger than my pinkie nail. A bright orange beamed around the sides and head, but it had brown and tan stripes all along its back, which looked like a sort of shell covering.

"They are Colorado potato beetles. We have to get rid of them or they will eat all the potato plants." I searched too, and together we added bugs to the can-of-no-return.

Suddenly, I spotted a small red creature eating a hole in a leaf. "Delmer, what's this?"

"Oh, no, that's one of the babies that already hatched. They cause more damage than the adults! We've got to find all of them!" Imagining life without potatoes and gravy and lefse, I worked extra hard. The nymphs varied in size and had a couple lines of black spots along their rounded backs. What we couldn't pick off, we squished.

"This is just disgusting!" I squeezed my eyes shut with each murder.

"We'll have to do this every day so they don't take over."

About a week later I followed Mom and my sisters to the garden. They each carried a bucket. We stooped over the pea plants. Plump pods protruded from the upper growth. "Make sure you hold onto the plant with your other hand as you pick," Mom taught. "Then more peas will come on if you are gentle."

It took a lot of peas for the family, so when we dumped four pailfuls on the kitchen table, even the men took time to help shuck.

Later that day, Mom carried another bucket out to the potato patch. She chose a tall plant with several blossoms on top and dug around in the soil at the base. Soon her nimble fingers brought forth a golf ball sized red potato. She kept working until she had enough for a meal for the family. I asked her why she didn't just dig the plant. "We want the rest of the potatoes to keep growing." I bet she was thinking of mashed potatoes and lefse too!

That night for supper we had peas (with cream) and new potatoes cooked in their "jackets." There is something wonderful about the combination. Dad summed it up as he scraped up the last forkful. "That's fit for a king!" The rest of us thought so too.

Chapter 45

Write Like Crazy!

It was a list of names. Following each, in perfect handwriting, was an address and notes of interest: hobbies, favorite animal. "Please choose someone from the list for your summer pen pal." Mrs. Sprang, our second-grade teacher, had exchanged student lists with a friend and was hoping we would practice our newly acquired penmanship skills.

It was fun getting letters from my pen pal that summer, but nothing compared to the many hand-written notes I received later in life. Dad sent us postcards when he and Mom traveled. Mom seemed to understand how a letter could remedy the homesickness felt by her child at Bible Camp. Later, when I had moved miles away, my heart soared when I found a letter in the mailbox from Mom, Aunt Julia or one of my sisters. I didn't need to look at the return address. I recognized their unique, beautiful-to-me handwriting.

The folks always wrote in cursive, though we didn't call it cursive then. When "please print" was indicated, they used block letters, and I could tell it didn't come easily. I don't remember asking, but wonder today if on our mother's very first day of country school the teacher commanded, "Get out your slates. Today we learn longhand!" I have saved letters and signatures from my parents and I treasure them. Even today, getting a letter from one of my siblings is a treat.

Deloris, Donald and Darlene started out in country school. Their teachers put great stock in neat handwriting. Later, in public school, Dorothy, Delmer and I continued with penmanship and practice of curlicues and loops and downstrokes. Our own children carried on the tradition. Lovely (or unique) letters joined to form expressions which spoke more than words; they drew a picture of the person who created them.

But times change as times do. In 2010, the revised Common Core State Standards for education did not include cursive handwriting. The majority of states adopted the new standards, thus removing the requirement for cursive instruction.

In this era of digital technology, handwriting is being erased from our lives. Consider the implications. Will our great-grandchildren be able to decipher the perfectly-penned words of the Declaration of Independence and the Bill of Rights? Will they be able to decode the calligraphic signature of John Hancock? Even more importantly, will the next generation be able to read those long-ago letters from Grandma?

Unfortunately, far more will be blotted from lives than lovely curlicues. Research reveals that the act of writing by hand has major cognitive benefits. It leads to higher levels of brain activity in regions responsible for movement, vision, sensory processing and memory. When we write something, our brains are actively engaged, thus we are more likely to understand and retain the information. Connecting all those squiggles and lines is cardio for the mind!

Engaging right and left brain, longhand stimulates creativity in young and old. Putting pen to paper can have a calming effect. Furthermore, what better way to leave a tangible connection with a loved one than the personal touch of a hand-written note?

How can we leave a trail with a fading art form? We can write! Literally, cross those t's and dot those i's. Write letters to loved ones. Pen important events in the family Bible. Keep a journal. Write about floods and drought and life.

Maybe someday our great-great-great grandchildren will find these heartfelt missives and study, research and translate all those strokes and squiggles. Could be they will say, "Those people who lived in the 2020's had super talents. They used some sort of tools to draw letters on a flat substance that originated from a tree. And they sure knew how to write good stories!"

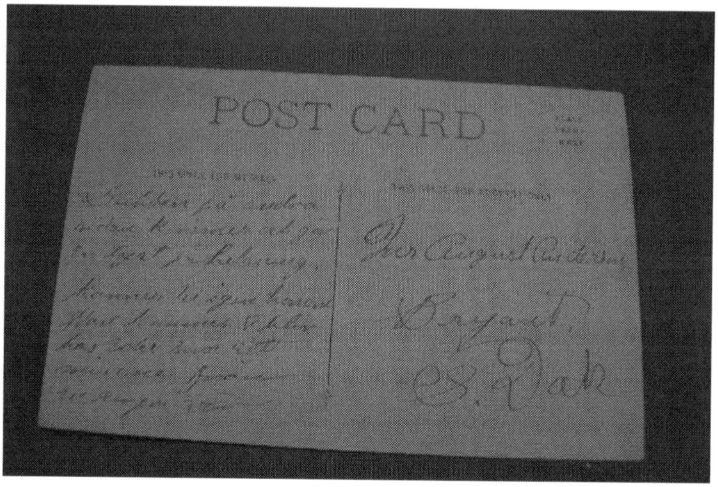

An old postcard from Sweden

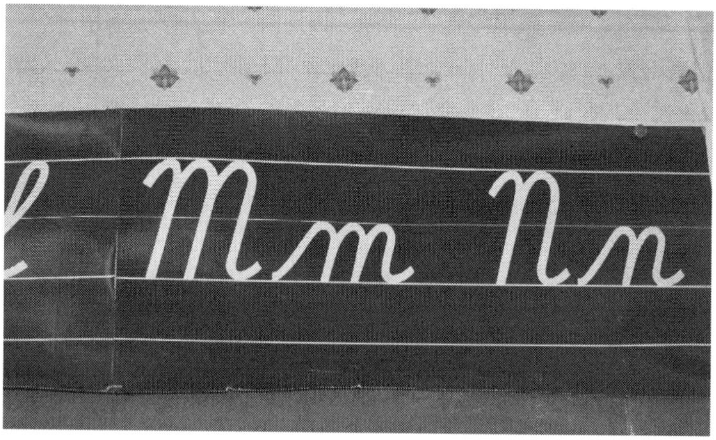

Cursive letters over the blackboard at the Harrison County Museum Schoolhouse

Chapter 46

The Unforgettable Lure of Danger

The sound of rushing water grew steadily louder as we approached. My short legs whirled as I tried to keep up. Just ahead, my brother slammed the pedals back and leaned left. His rear tire skidded, then slid to the right as the front tire continued its journey to the very edge. The edge of the four-foot cement culvert that now contained a raging river. The edge between solid ground and foaming, muddy water that crashed through the rocks below and fanned out into the field.

The culvert went under the gravel road just north of our farm. It allowed water to drain from the neighbor's field to ours, forming what we called the crick. Most of the time the crick was a gentle stream or maybe even a trickle, depending on Mother Nature. A four-inch deluge the night before fed in more water than the channel could hold.

I footed down my kickstand on the side of the road and cautiously approached Delmer as he stood astride his red Roadmaster. We watched the water rushing at our feet, taking in the earthy-fresh scent and the fighting waves. Suddenly, my brother got off his bike and shimmied to the rim, dangling his feet over Niagara Falls! "Come on, DeAnn. This is so cool."

Like a moth drawn to a flame, I baby-stepped next to him. My heart pounded like a sledge hammer, but I bent one knee, then the other and there I was, experiencing a fear-fought moment that is still etched in my brain.

A lifetime later I started out on Highway 30 after work. Snowmelt and heavy rains had swollen nearby rivers and streams. There was talk of closing roads and bridges. If I was going to be stranded, I wanted it to be at home. I turned off 30 and approached the Boyer Bridge. I gasped at the lake before me. Fields were flooded on all sides. The water flowed dangerously close to the bottom of the bridge. Logs and other debris lifted and fell into the depths.

On the other side of the bridge two cars waited. One was a Sheriff's vehicle. I stopped before crossing, but the deputy motioned me forward. On the other side I pulled over well ahead of the other cars. The officers informed me that the bridge was still safe. I asked about taking pictures, as I stared at the expanse of water, the road sign jutting from the surface. "Sure. You can walk right out on the bridge." The deputy smiled just a little. It was not a challenge, but more of a Lady-you-don't-know-what-you're-in-for grin. I grabbed my Nikon and strode bravely toward the bridge. I clicked away. The farther out I walked onto the bridge, the more eerie things became. The structure creaked and groaned. Every few seconds I heard (and felt) clunks below me. I sweated as I imagined logs pounding into the bridge's underwater supports, but I was certain that the best photos would be from the very middle. The structure seemed to vibrate as the watery inferno surged below. I will never forget those few seconds.

As humans, we are sometimes drawn to danger. We face it, confront our fears and extend our boundaries. There is something powerful and transforming that happens within us. Is this lure of the unknown the reason photo journalists risk their lives to get that award-winning photo? Or reporters enter war zones? Is it why the words "tornado warning" thrill storm chasers? Is it what brought our ancestors to America? Is it what drives researchers to seek a cure for cancer?

To leave a trail, we may also need to confront fear and push boundaries. I am not saying we should cross the Atlantic on a surfboard or ride a motorcycle over 50 cars. (Remember Evel Knievel?)

But sometimes life might be calling us to get out of our comfort zones. To reach out to an estranged relative. Pray for someone we despise. To learn something new. We may find an unknown inner strength. We may experience unforgettable moments.

"Twenty years from now you will be more disappointed by the things you didn't do than by the ones you did. So...sail away from the safe harbour... Explore. Dream. Discover." Mark Twain knew how to leave a trail.

Chapter 47

It's Great When It Works!

Silence is golden. But not when you are waiting to hear the sound of your washer kick in. I had pulled out the button on my Kenmore, turned it to the maximum wash time and pushed Start. Water began pouring in, so I added detergent and a load of light-colored items. I would hang out the cleaned, rinsed and spun laundry when the washer was done. But the washer did not get done. It stopped when the water reached the appropriate level and then nothing. When I did not hear the typical swirls and spins, I opened the machine. The lovely lavender scent of the detergent greeted me, but the t-shirts and unmentionables floated in the same places I had dropped them.

Hmmm. I fiddled with the knobs. Tried resetting at a different speed or time. Nothing made it suddenly kick in. I scooted to the basement to check the breaker box. No breakers were broken. I noticed that the door-activated on/off switch in the little hole under the cover seemed to be askew. Nothing to be done but call for help.

The good man at my favorite appliance store informed me

that their repair people were swamped. When I asked him how soon I could hope for repair, he replied, "It won't be this week."

I got to thinking that sweet lavender smell might change to stink weed if I left those clothes to brew for a week. Visions of our mother's washboard danced in my head. It hung on the wall over the wringer-washer in our old porch. My siblings and I all remember Mom pulling that rough board down to use occasionally, but she never assigned the task to any of us. We didn't question it at the time, but figured she had her reasons.

A washboard would have come in handy for my present-day dilemma, along with a tub and a way to transfer the water to it. I remembered emptying Mom's wringer-washer by simply unhooking the nozzle which was attached to a hose and lowering it over a bucket; good old gravity never fails.

I ended up swishing the clothes around in the water by hand, then fishing the items out one by one, squeezing out some of the water and plopping them into a five-gallon bucket. I then filled the bucket with cold water from my outside faucet. I lifted and dipped each item a few times and then hung them, dripping wet, on the clothesline. It took a few trips, but finally everything was rinsing and dripping and drying out in the sun.

My memories again floated back to our growing up years. Our mother loved her wringer-washer. I clearly remember her saying, "I like to wash clothes." I questioned how anyone could like anything that was so much work.

Looking back, I wonder if Mom grew up using a washboard. Bending over big old metal tubs, she and her sisters probably scrubbed their large family's wash every week. They would have rubbed every item from hanky to diaper to overalls over the rough metal surface, scrubbing out the dirt. Then they rinsed them in another tub and squeezed out the water the best they could. For sure, Mom started married life with only a washboard until she saved up enough to buy her wash machine.

Now I understand why Mom enjoyed doing the laundry with her new-fangled wringer-washer, and why she didn't ask her children to use that old washboard—not even once.

One good thing about a washboard, though: it never broke down.

CHAPTER 47

Washboard at Harrison County Museum

Chapter 48

Horsepower, Brainpower and Integrity

Black smoke puffed from the exhaust pipe of the Farmall as it waited at the starting line. The driver focused intently on the contest director 70 yards ahead as the man on the loudspeaker announced the first weight class. The crowd grew silent and moved closer to the ropes. Only the "weight riders" were allowed inside the ropes, close to the track. Mom and I stood among the crowd of spectators half way to the end of the sod path.

Suddenly, the director dropped the white flag and the red machine lurched forward. The De Smet Tractor Pulling Contest had begun! The Farmall pulled a flat metal skid. On both sides of the track men stood at designated spots. As the skid moved by, a man on one side stepped on, then one on the other side, gradually adding weight. The powerful engine pulled a bit harder as its load increased, but it kept chugging along. All at once, the tires started spinning and digging. The director flashed his red flag. The farmer pulled back the clutch to stop and his tractor resumed its regular pulse. The crowd cheered and clapped. Officials hurried in to measure the distance pulled.

With the first performance duly recorded, the weight guys returned to their places and the tractor pulled forward. At the edge of the track, the driver waited while workers unhooked the skid to be pulled back to the starting line by a small tractor. The farmer walked back to the field. Dad and the other upcoming contestants gathered around him. I watched them slap him on the back and shake his hand. He nodded his thanks and made a comment. Laughter floated to the crowd.

Soon the next tractor waited at the start line and the contest continued. Dad drew the fourth position that day. He had explained to me that there's an advantage to be one of the first drivers because the track gets broken up with each run. Mom and I had moved closer to the finish line when it was Dad's turn, hopeful that he would pull farther than the others. Her hand rested on my shoulder.

The John Deere 3020 sparkled in the South Dakota sun as it purred at the start line. Dad had taken the hose and chamois to it when he brought it in from the field last night. The flag dropped and Dad was off! Maybe it was my dad-hero imagination, but to me he was moving a bit faster than the first three. The weight guys piled on as the Deere moved down the track. It passed the torn-up dirt from the first tractor. It continued farther than the others so far. The men kept stepping onto the skid closer and closer to the director. All at once, the front end lifted a few inches off the ground. I held my breath and Mom's fingers tightened on my shoulder. Dad's hand gripped the throttle, his eyes glued to the director. The engine quavered just a bit and the front wheels circled needlessly in the air, but the 3020 forged on.

Dad won the tractor pull that day and placed in various

contests over a span of years during the 1960s. His trophies filled the top of the book case. Our brother Donald also got caught up in the Tractor Pull excitement. He excelled with the 4020 in a different class.

I remember asking our father what he did to win, expecting some complicated adjustment that increased horsepower. He explained that driving skill was the most important factor; the driver had to learn what gear and speed worked best.

In those contests, regular farmers brought their regular tractors to compete. "Pull on Sunday, plow on Monday." Later the contests evolved into modified machines that were used only for competition. Engines were added. Tractors that no longer resembled tractors became dragsters. Such machines still thrill crowds at power pulling contests across the nation.

Times change, but I hope that there are still little girls and boys who cheer for their dad and think he is the best no matter what. I hope that when the drivers finish, the others all gather around them, pat their backs and shake their hands. I hope they still laugh.

Dad with trophy after tractor pulling contest

Chapter 49

Practice Makes Perfect

The term "lazy days of summer" did not apply to the middle months on the farm. The family was busy "making hay while the sun shines," and "sweating it out" in the kitchen. Along with the farm and garden demands of the season we all added getting ready for the fair.

The county fair as we know it began in 1811. A man named Elkanah Watson from New York raised Merino sheep on his farm and wanted to improve agriculture. He formed a society that organized an annual livestock exhibition. Farmers earned prize money for the best oxen, sheep, cattle and hogs. Later the group included crops. The concept spread across the East and Midwest through the nineteenth century, continuing the purpose of agricultural education.

Involving young people in programs (the seed of 4-H) came about later. Early "hands-on" programs connected public education with country life. Youth clubs began. Many were project oriented like "Corn Clubs" and "Canning Clubs." Jessie Field Shambaugh, from Shenandoah, Iowa, developed a clover pin with an H on each leaf, and by 1912, groups were called 4-H clubs.

The Kingsbury County Fair in De Smet, South Dakota was, and still is, called Achievement Days. A huge part of the fair involves 4-H projects and activities. The Head, Heart, Hands and Health organization impacted the lives of all six of us kids and our parents.

Goals set during the winter came to fruition in summer. Projects needed to be created, practiced or polished. We all aimed for the highest awards possible, hopefully purple ribbons. Because purple ribbons earned a place at the State Fair and everyone wanted to enter at the State Fair!

The girls in our family were encouraged to participate in Foods and Nutrition. For some reason, all four of us chose to exhibit banana bread at least once during our 4-H careers. Our leaders and our mothers taught us that "practice makes perfect," so when bananas on the counter grew spots, we practiced. The best learned lessons are the goofs, and believe me, we had them. Too brown on the bottom. A little doughy in the center.

The family were our taste testers, so for days, the dark-flecked, golden (hopefully) slices added to our supper and snack menus. Always the encourager, Dad raved about every loaf. Even after the fourth daughter's trials (and errors) he applauded: "Delicious! Best banana bread I ever tasted!"

Our 4-H leaders challenged us to try new things and do demonstrations. "If you win a purple on a demonstration, you get to stay at the fair!"

Deloris was barely 10 when she took on the challenge. Her project was creating different kinds of milk drinks. She came up with chocolate and strawberry. The Extension Agent, Miss Sloat, suggested another flavor, something unique and healthier. "How about molasses?" Deloris experimented with her recipes and practiced.

Our sister presented her dairy demonstration at Achievement Days and won a purple ribbon. She was excited and nervous when she advanced to the South Dakota State Fair in Huron a few weeks later. The demonstration area was in the old army barracks. The large room held only a table for the exhibitor, the judge's area, and a few folding chairs for observers. On the big day, Deloris set up her table with only Mom, Dad and her younger siblings at the time, Donald, Darlene and Dorothy in the audience.

She mixed the three beverages and explained what she was doing. She hailed the health benefits of milk. Finally, she took samples to the judge to taste. The woman tested each and nodded her approval. She asked questions and Deloris responded. About the time the girl was relieved to be done, the judge turned to the family. She smiled at Donald. The eight-year-old was beyond ready to get back out to the fair and climb on the green tractors. "Young man, do you like your sister's milk drinks?"

Donald wrinkled his nose and slowly shook his head. Little did he know he had ten years of banana bread trials awaiting him!

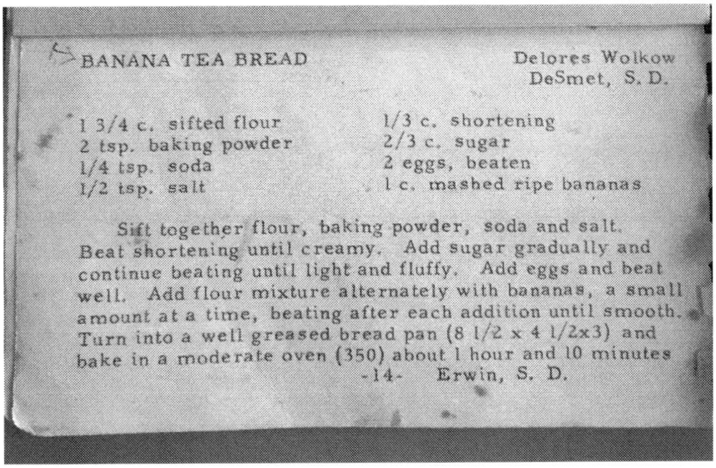

BANANA TEA BREAD

Delores Wolkow
DeSmet, S. D.

1 3/4 c. sifted flour	1/3 c. shortening
2 tsp. baking powder	2/3 c. sugar
1/4 tsp. soda	2 eggs, beaten
1/2 tsp. salt	1 c. mashed ripe bananas

Sift together flour, baking powder, soda and salt. Beat shortening until creamy. Add sugar gradually and continue beating until light and fluffy. Add eggs and beat well. Add flour mixture alternately with bananas, a small amount at a time, beating after each addition until smooth. Turn into a well greased bread pan (8 1/2 x 4 1/2x3) and bake in a moderate oven (350) about 1 hour and 10 minutes

-14- Erwin, S. D.

Recipe from the Erwin cookbook

Chapter 50

Made With Hands and Heart

The battered metal dishpan rocked on the kitchen table. Dents rounded the bottom, but the pan glistened in the light, polished from years of use. Mom poured liquid from the saucepan she brought from the stove; she had drained and saved the cooking water from last night's potatoes.

"Potato water makes the bread taste better and helps the yeast work." Mom's long wooden spoon hummed pleasantly as it glided over the bottom of the big pan. Likely, she was thinking her youngest daughter would carry on the bread-baking tradition.

Mom dipped her finger in the liquid. "If it's too hot, it will kill the yeast and the bread won't rise."

Satisfied that the liquid was the Goldilocks standard, "just right," Mom sprinkled several packages of yeast over the top. While the yeast "proofed" we gathered ingredients. She plopped a dollop of shortening into the warm saucepan. I lugged bags of dark flour to the table—rye and whole wheat. Mom called the wheat "graham" flour. She found salt, sugar and a bottle of Brer Rabbit molasses. I scooped white flour from the bin into a bowl.

Knees on a chair and elbows on the table, I watched. Mom dumped white flour into the yeast mixture and stirred. She dumped in a bit of sugar. A thick, stream of molasses darkened the batter and smelled wonderful. She scooped in some dark flour.

"Don't you need to measure it?"

"I do measure—with my hands." Mom smiled. She poured a bit of salt into her hand and sprinkled it in. Soon the melted shortening disappeared into the depths of the dark dough. "Salt and fat can hinder the yeast. That's why we added flour first."

Mom mixed in more flour until the dough became stiff and I wondered how she could even stir it. Hands took over for the spoon. She pulled dough in from one side, then another, folding over each time and pushing back.

"Kneading gives bread a fine texture," Mom taught.

"How long do you knead it?" It seemed to me like she would never get done.

"I can tell by how the dough feels when it is ready."

At last, she stopped kneading. She gave it one last pat, covered it with a dish towel and set it near the stove.

"We'll let that rise until it doubles."

In less than an hour the dish towel grew to a small mountain. Mom let me punch the dough down. "You need to get all the air out, then we let it rise again. This makes the bread tender."

Soon it was time to make the dough into loaves. We greased pans. Mom split the dough into five chunks. She pressed each one flat on her giant wooden board, then sprinkled on raisins.

"Delmer loves raisin bread." Mom smiled as she formed and patted loaves into pans. Again, the bread rose, snuggled under the towel.

When five little hills pushed up the towel, Mom preheated the oven. Soon she spaced the loaves on the oven shelf and closed the door. In minutes a glorious scent filled the kitchen. We cleaned the table, got ingredients put away and washed and dried dishes.

Mom must have had a built-in timer; she opened the oven door, reached in and knocked on a loaf with her fist. Within seconds, five golden loaves cooled on the table. I rubbed butter over the tops with a scrap of wax paper.

After a few minutes, Mom cut two slices from one of the loaves. Butter melted into the raisin-flecked softness. Together, we savored our reward.

Memories of this piece of heaven are sweet—of our mother who baked with her hands and her heart.

Mom with a loaf of fresh bread

Some of Mom's pans. Thanks to niece Susan for photo.

Chapter 51

A Walk to Remember

Screams of fright drowned out the bellow of a distraught cow in the distance. A discordant chorus of humans and machines bombarded us from all sides as we hurried to our destination. A calliope whistled loudly as plastic horses rose and fell on the Merry-Go-Round. The Ferris Wheel squeaked as a tub halted and rocked over the platform. Flags flapped in the wind and tent tops flumped up and down. A loud clang echoed as the sledgehammer hit its mark. The bell rang above us and the man in the booth challenged onlookers to outdo the strongest man.

"Step right up!" "Win a teddy bear for your sweetheart!" Barkers called from their stalls. People stopped. Watched. Talked. Laughed. Some reached for their pocketbooks. Others like us plodded on.

Pink and green neon lights flashed in the near-darkness; cars spun and lifted on the Tilt-a-Whirl. Golden bulbs beckoned in front of kiosks. Signs and bizarre pictures grabbed my attention. "Toss a dime and win a plate." "Get your fortune read. Only $1.00." "See the world's only living two-headed pig!" "Bearded Lady!"

Interspersed with the entertainment areas were food places. "Hotdog on a stick!" (I thought sadly of the adorable flop-eared critters in the hog barn.) Places sold funnel cakes, caramel apples and cotton candy. I knew better than to ask Dad for cotton candy. His standard reply: "Rots your teeth out."

We had just finished supper out in the parking lot. Mom had packed fried chicken, homemade buns and apple pie. I was not hungry, but my tummy rumbled just the same. The spicy-cinnamon, salty-dog, and burnt sugar aromas blended and tickled my nostrils with a unique, intoxicating scent: State Fair Anticipation.

It seemed like Dad started walking faster. (Maybe his tummy rumbled too!) Mom, Darlene, Dorothy and I had to scramble to keep up with him and Delmer.

"We're almost there," Dad lifted the dark green army blanket draped over his arm to check his watch. He smiled at Mom and their small caravan as we got in line in front of the grandstand.

A young usher glanced at our tickets and led the way up steps and through folded seats to our places. Dad bought three big boxes of popcorn from a vendor in a funny white hat.

The crowd filled in all around us and I could feel the excitement. Below us brightly-colored clowns with Rudolf noses carried barrels out on the field. Cowboys in Stetsons straddled wooden fences, ropes curled in their gloved hands. Broncos kicked and bucked, hating being confined to pens. Bulls snorted and bawled, pawing the ground. The cool evening breeze carried in a country song. Mom spread the heavy blanket over our laps and I snuggled cozily between her and Dad.

Suddenly, five teenage girls in sequin-coated Western outfits rode to the center of the arena and stopped. Their beautiful horses bowed heads and knelt in unison before the American flag. The clear strong voice of the announcer blared through the speakers above us.

"Welcome to the South Dakota State Fair Rodeo!"

At that moment I knew I had to be the luckiest little girl alive.

Chapter 52

Waste Not, Want Not

"The golden-rod is yellow;
The corn is turning brown;
The trees in apple orchards
With fruit are bending down."

Mom could recite the whole poem, "September," by Helen Hunt Jackson. I always get stuck after the fruit bending down line. When the fruit bowed the branches on our apple trees on the farm, our mother made sure we put it to good use.

The crab apples ripened first, but if green ones fell to the ground, we were on it. The folks planted those trees early in their married life. Mom had no doubt that God did make the little green apples and they were a precious gift. Jars of juice soon lined basement shelves and would be relished in cold months ahead. As the pink and green pomes ripened, juice dripped down our chins as we filled buckets. Mom's apple pickles would sparkle with the pickled beets and beans on the Sunday relish tray.

Delmer remembers seeing the blue Ford pickup pull in and wait at the end of the stubble field. The John Deere 730 finished a round and Dad walked out to meet his young son. He grinned as he emptied six crab apples from his overall pockets. Our brother munched on them through the afternoon as the four-bottom plow turned over the black dirt behind him.

As the later fall apples ripened, baking and preserving began in earnest. Apple crisp, cake, bars and muffins. Baked apples provided the perfect dessert. Mom cut out the cores and placed the fruit in a glass cake pan. A sprinkling of sugar and cinnamon over the top created a sweet syrup at the bottom. Still warm from the oven, with a crown of whipped cream, baked apples made an easy delicious dessert.

Mom lined slices of fruit on cookie sheets to dry in the oven. She carefully cut rings from large, unblemished fruit and cooked them with melted Red-hots to make candied apples for Christmas.

A huge kettle of apple butter simmered on the back burner on a cool fall day, the spicy aroma making our mouths water. And if you give a kid apple butter, she will want homemade bread to go with it!

When peeling was required, the girls all took our turns. A bowl of water waited with lemon juice in it. "Keeps the apples from turning brown," Mother taught. I remember trying to keep the peel in one complete spiral without breaking it. It didn't matter if they were broken when we cooked them for juice for jelly. "The peels contain pectin. Pectin makes jelly set up." Mom smiled at the bounty of jars on the counter, especially when she heard the distinctive clicks of the seals popping.

When our folks got married, our mother continued her family's tradition of baking pies for Sunday dinner. Apple pies were a favorite, so we peeled and sliced and packed into jars. In winter Mom used the canned apples for pies. She said they weren't as good as fresh, but we never complained. That same sweet, spicy syrup trickled onto our plates as we sank our forks into the flaky crust.

Dad and the boys joined in the pursuit of preservation. When a hard frost threatened, they set up the ladder and picked from the high branches. Baskets of red striped fruit waited in the porch to be wrapped in newspaper and packed away in a cool room.

One year, when there was a particularly heavy crop, Mom tried her hand at apple jack. The concoction fermented down in the basement. Mom's sisters teased her about her home brew. They laughed until tears rolled down their faces. Strangely enough, none of us kids got to sample the beverage.

Having lived through hard times, the folks believed that nothing should be wasted. They had learned to store food in years of plenty because the next year may be lean. None of us complained those years when the trees were "bending down" with fruit. Likely, we could smell the apple pie!

Many apple pies were baked in this lovely pan. Thank you, Susan, for the photo!

Chapter 53

Keep the Stories Coming!

Eight of us sat around the long wooden table. The supper conversation had centered around the Erwin basketball team, tomorrow night's game and Donald's "great shots" last Friday night.

"You couldn't miss!" Delmer exclaimed proudly. Donald grinned, but quietly accepted the praise from his little brother.

Mom stood to get the coffee. Dad scraped the last smidgen of apple pie from his plate and leaned back contentedly in his chair. Secret glances passed among the kids, for we knew a story was coming; we knew we had heard it before.

"I was just a freshman. We were behind ten points at half time. The other team had a six-foot-four center that just kept dumping in baskets.

"The coach looked at me in the huddle. 'Do you think you can stop that big guy?'

"I told him, 'If I can't do it, you don't have anybody who can.'

"The guy didn't score the whole second half."

Stories often added to our family's supper menu when we

grew up. No TV or radio noises competed. We stayed in our places until everyone was finished, conversation completed and it was time to do dishes. It was the perfect opportunity to pass down memories.

Riding in the car on Sunday afternoons with no particular destination, we drove by an abandoned old house. "I worked there one summer as a hired girl," Mom recalled. "The family had seven young kids."

Dad pointed out what was left of a homestead. "They lost their farm in The Depression." Dad's eyes met Mom's. We could feel the sadness in the back seat. "Lots of farms went under then."

Mid-afternoon lunch in the shade of the tractor tire provided another good talking time. Mom had filled a small pail with sandwiches and cookies and instructed me to walk to the end of the oat field and wait for Dad to come around. He smiled and waved me forward. On those visits, among the songs of birds and crickets, I learned about the grandma I never knew, how she died and how sad Dad was.

There is something about the swish of hot water, the clatter of silver and the soft rub of white cotton over plates that is conducive to conversation. As Mom washed and I dried, I learned about my mother's days in country school, the stern teacher and her insistence that Mom not write with her preferred left hand.

As I knelt next to Mom's chair in the living room, she paged through an old photo album. Mom pointed to my great-grandparents who immigrated from Sweden and built a sod house where our Grandma Selma was born.

Our parents often told us stories as we were growing up; it seemed there were plenty of quiet moments, opportunities to talk and listen.

But times have changed. Do families still sit and talk around the supper table without competition from some kind of screen? Whatever happened to Sunday drives? Do children carry lunch to their parent who is working out in the field? Do they take the time to sit in the shade and talk? Have automatic dishwashers diminished communications between parent and child? Have photo albums become a thing of the past? If we don't print pictures, what tangible evidence do we have of lives lived?

We each have our own stories, our unique roles in history. If the stories are not passed on to others, to another generation, then that part of history dies when our earthly lives end.

I wish I would have listened more carefully to our parents' and brother's stories. I wish I would have asked them questions and begged for more details. We cannot go back. But we can pass along the stories we know of our ancestors. We can record and tell our own stories to our children and grandchildren. We must keep the stories coming!

About the Author

DeAnn (Wolkow) Kruempel grew up on a farm near De Smet, South Dakota, the sixth child of Harrison and Mabel Wolkow. She attended school at Erwin and De Smet. She married Vicar Robert Kruempel and lived in Benedict, North Dakota, and Toeterville, Akron, and Missouri Valley, Iowa.

The author worked in school and public libraries for more than 30 years before retiring in 2022. She now resides on an acreage near Logan, Iowa, loving her time with children and grandchildren as well as her orchard, gardens, honeybees and chickens.

Kruempel's siblings, who are often the characters in the stories, share their memories and the author blends them into heart-warming tales with adventure, humor, love and hope. She brings history to life in her unique writing style. All of DeAnn Kruempel's works promote strong family values and are enjoyed by all ages.

You can connect with me on:

- https://www.amazon.com/author/deannkruempel
- https://www.facebook.com/deann.kruempel.1

Also by DeAnn (Wolkow) Kruempel

Other books by DeAnn Kruempel:

Promises to Keep

Promises Challenged

Promises Strengthened

Promises in Courage

Promises Under Fire

Once Upon a Midwest Sunset

Putting on the Big Boots

Back to Forward

The author's first five books are a historical fiction series about a young family as they follow their dreams of having their own farm in the late 1930s. The novels begin after The Great Depression and continue through the end of World War II. Share tears with the Andersson family as they endure fire, drought, polio, influenza and more. Rejoice in their triumphs as love, courage and devotion pull them through. Laugh at the antics of the unforgettable characters.

Once Upon a Midwest Sunset, *Putting on the Big Boots* and *Back to Forward* are compilations of the stories from her newspaper columns each year since they begin in 2020.

Back to Forward
Kruempel's third book of stories from her newspaper column that appears in newspapers across the Midwest. The often humorous stories blend the memories of the author and her siblings. Many are of their years of growing up on the family farm in South Dakota.

Made in the USA
Columbia, SC
10 October 2024

44119585R00107